T0213123

Lecture Notes of the Institute
for Computer Sciences, Social Informatics
and Telecommunications Engineering   107

Andreas U. Schmidt   Giovanni Russello
Ioannis Krontiris   Shiguo Lian (Eds.)

Security and Privacy in Mobile Information and Communication Systems

4th International Conference, MobiSec 2012
Frankfurt am Main, Germany, June 25-26, 2012
Revised Selected Papers

 Springer

Volume Editors

Andreas U. Schmidt
Novalyst IT AG, Robert-Bosch Str. 38
61184 Karben, Germany
E-mail: andreas.schmidt@novalyst.de

Giovanni Russello
University of Auckland, Department of Computer Science
Private Bag 92019, Auckland 1142, New Zealand
E-mail: g.russello@auckland.ac.nz

Ioannis Krontiris
Deutsche Telekom, Mobile Business and Multilateral Security
Grüneburgplatz 1, 60629 Frankfurt/Main, Germany
E-mail: ioannis.krontiris@m-chair.net

Shiguo Lian
Central Research Institute Huawei Technologies
Building Q22, Beiqinglu Huanbaoyuan No.156,
Haidian District, Beijing 100095, China
E-mail: shiguo.lian@ieee.org

ISSN 1867-8211   e-ISSN 1867-822X
ISBN 978-3-642-33391-0   ISBN 978-3-642-33392-7 (eBook)
DOI 10.1007/978-3-642-33392-7

Springer Heidelberg Dordrecht London New York

Library of Congress Control Number: 2012946629

CR Subject Classification (1998): C.5.3, K.6.5, C.2.0, C.2.2-5, H.4, K.4.4, J.1, C.3

Typesetting: Camera-ready by author, data conversion by Scientific Publishing Services, Chennai, India

Printed on acid-free paper

Springer is part of Springer Science+Business Media (www.springer.com)

Preface

On behalf of the organizing committee, it is our pleasure to welcome you to Frankfurt am Main, to the fourth ICST conference on security and privacy for mobile information and communication systems (MobiSec 2012). MobiSec 2012 covers some of the most active areas of research in mobile security. The focus areas of this year's conference are all on the application side of security, highlighting the practical importance of security of mobile devices in concrete usages. The topics covered by MobiSec 2012 range from user privacy issues, over mobile application and App security, to mobile identity management, and NFC. With its orientation toward applications, MobiSec constitutes a perfect interface between academia and industry in the field of mobile communications.

Highlights of MobiSec 2012 are the three keynotes by our renowned keynote speakers Amardeo Sarma, Kai Rannenberg, and Kim Cameron. Amardeo Sarma's keynote explores the balance between privacy and trust in digital societies under the impact of paradigm-shifting new technologies such as M2M communication and the cloud. Kai Rannenberg talks about how to reconcile privacy with user-friendly identity management, based on mobile devices as trustworthy platforms. Kim Cameron rounds off the keynotes with his view on why the cloud makes it necessary to redefine what we mean by identity management.

Many people contributed to the organization of MobiSec. It was a privilege to work with these dedicated persons, and we would like to thank them all for their efforts. The Organizing Committee as a whole created a frictionless, collaborative work atmosphere, which made our task an easy one. A high-quality conference cannot be created without the help of the distinguished members of the Program Committee, overseen by the TPC chairs Ioannis Kontiris and Giovanni Russello.

Thanks go to all other members of the Organizing Committee: Shiguo Lian (Publications Chair), Andreas Leicher (Web Chair), and in particular to Flaminia Luccio for soliciting and overseeing keynotes. The support of the conference organizer, ICST, represented by Aza Swedin and Justina Senkus of the European Alliance for Innovation, is greatly acknowledged. Finally, we would like to thank Imrich Chlamtac and the members of the Steering Committee for their support and guidance during these months.

Concluding, we hope you find MobiSec 2012 stimulating and thought-provoking.

July 2012

Andreas U. Schmidt
Neeli R. Prasad

Organization

Steering Committee

Imrich Chlamtac (Chair)	CREATE-NET Research Consortium, Trento, Italy
Ramjee Prasad	Aalborg University, Denmark
Andreas U. Schmidt	Novalyst IT AG, Karben, Germany

Organizing Committee

General Chair/General Co-chairs

Neeli R. Prasad	Aalborg University, Denmark
Andreas U. Schmidt	Novalyst IT AG, Karben, Germany

TPC Chair/TPC Co-chairs

Giovanni Russello	University of Auckland, New Zealand
Ioannis Krontiris	Goethe University Frankfurt, Germany

Publication Chair

Shiguo Lian	Huawei, China

Publicity Chair(s)

Rasmus Hjorth Nielsen	CTIF, Princeton, USA
Mauro Conti	University of Padua, Italy

Workshops Chair(s)

Vincent Naessens	KaHo Sint-Lieven, Gent, Belgium

Panels Chair

Dirk Kröselberg	Siemens CERT, Munich, Germany

Special Sessions, Keynotes and Panels Chair

Flaminia Luccio	Università Ca' Foscari, Venezia, Italy

Web Chair

Andreas Leicher	Novalyst IT AG, Karben, Germany

Technical Program Committee

Andreas Albers	Goethe University Frankfurt, Germany
Claudio Agostino Ardagna	University of Milan, Italy
Lejla Batina	Radboud University Nijmegen, The Netherlands
Zinaida Benenson	University of Erlangen-Nuremberg, Germany
Rocky Chang	Hong Kong Polytechnic University, China
Mauro Conti	University of Padua, Italy
Bruno Crispo	University of Trento, Italy
Tassos Dimitriou	Athens Information Technology, Greece
Changyu Dong	University of Strathclyde, UK
William Enck	North Carolina State University, USA
Hannes Federrath	University of Hamburg, Germany
Felix Freiling	University of Erlangen-Nuremberg, Germany
Ashish Gehani	SRI International, USA
Seda Gürses	Katholieke Universiteit Leuven, Belgium
Dogan Kesdogan	University of Siegen, Germany
Geir M. Køien	University of Adger, Norway
Marc Langheinrich	University of Lugano, Switzerland
Jiqiang Lu	Institute for Infocomm Research, Singapore
Flaminia Luccio	University Ca' Foscari of Venice, Italy
Emmanouil Magkos	Ionian University, Greece
Marco Casassa Mont	Hewlett Packard Laboratories, Bristol, UK
Raphael C.-W. Phan	Loughborough University, UK
Anand Prasad	NEC Laboratories Japan
Reijo Savola	VTT Technical Research Centre of Finland, Finland
Aubrey-Derrick Schmidt	TU Berlin, Germany
Jean-Pierre Seifert	TU Berlin, T-Labs, Germany
Elaine Shi	UC Berkeley, USA
Claudio Silvestri	University Ca' Foscari of Venice, Italy
Claudio Soriente	Universidad Politecnica de Madrid, Spain
Thorsten Strufe	University of Mannheim, Germany
Allan Tomlinson	Royal Holloway, University of London, UK
Martin Werner	Ludwig-Maximilians-Universität München, Germany

Table of Contents

APEFS: An Infrastructure for Permission-Based Filtering of Android Apps

Simon Meurer and Roland Wismüller

University of Siegen
{simon.meurer,roland.wismueller}@uni-siegen.de
http://www.bs.informatik.uni-siegen.de

Abstract. The mobile device market is booming. This gains among others from the growing of application markets for those devices. In Android the applications (apps) are controlled by permissions of what they are allowed to do. The problem here is that many users do not pay attention to these permissions because they are rather complex and the user is informed about them only shortly before installing an app. In this paper we present *APEFS*, an infrastructure that enables a user to filter apps by permissions *before* trying to install them. Thereby it simplifies the usage of the permission system by allowing users to think about security and privacy before even searching for an app. We also enhance *APEFS* to not only filter by permissions but also by possible information flows, using static information flow analysis combined with runtime assertions.

Keywords: Android, Permissions, Android Market, Google Play, Infrastructure, Filter, Information Flow Analysis.

1 Introduction

Android, developed by the Open Handset Alliance, is the most popular mobile platform for Smartphones worldwide [13]. The success of the platform gains among other things from the ever increasing number of third party applications available in Google Play (currently about 450,000 [15]).

However, security and especially privacy are still open issues with handheld devices. While the Apple App Store at least enforces a code review, Google Play is completely open, which further aggravates the problem. The permission system of Android is not a sufficient solution. One reason for this is the fact that the permissions requested by an app (e.g., call someone, send SMS, use internet connections) are presented to the user only just before installation. So a user possibly first searches for an app to find out later that it uses a features the user doesn't want to grant. As an example, a user may search for a live wallpaper and finds apps that want to use phone calls and send SMS with costs. In the top 500 free live wallpapers on Google Play we found 10 apps that use phone calls and 4 apps that want to send SMS.

To get an impression on how many users actually do not inspect the permissions an app requests, we have developed two LiveWallpapers (Cyber Tennis and

A.U. Schmidt et al. (Eds.): MOBISEC 2012, LNICST 107, pp. 1–11, 2012.

Brick Breaking), where Cyber Tennis requests about 20 permissions including "internet", "send SMS", and "access location", and Brick Breaking requests *all* permissions that are available. Of course, both apps actually do not use any of these permissions. We proved that by using Stowaway[11], a tool which identifies unused permissions. The result for our apps was, that all permissions are unnecessary. After five months in Google Play, we have counted over 5,400 installations of both apps (about 3,300 for Cyber Tennis) and even got very positive ratings. We received no complaint whatsoever about the apps' permissions. This means that when an interesting app has been found, a significant number of users does not care about its permissions at all.

We think that this result is at least partially caused by a wrong approach, which first lets a user search for an app and only then presents him the permissions that this app requests. The permissions are only shown in a separate window that the user can quickly ignore by just pressing an accept button. So the user typically will not inspect the permissions and just installs the app.

Our approach gives more power to the permissions by first letting the user set his security level and then search only for apps that fit this level. We implemented APEFS (Android PErmission Filter System), an infrastructure that enables a user to filter apps by the permissions he wants to grant to the apps. In addition, it allows users to use predefined security profiles for certain classes of apps or create their own profiles.

While in this way the permissions are strengthened because they are not only another item to accept, just restricting the permissions is often not sufficient. As an example, consider a user searching for a cost-free contact manager app. Such apps often are financed via advertisements loaded from the internet, so it is clear that the app will need both the "read contacts" and "internet" permissions. Nevertheless, it should not be allowed to publish all the contacts in the internet. Thus, we need a method to determine (and enforce) the possible information flow in an app, which enables a corresponding filtering. We are currently enhancing APEFS with a tool for static information flow analysis, which finds out what the apps actually do with the permissions they request.

The rest of the paper is organized as follows: Section 2 describes the basics of Androids permission system and the software platform Google Play. Section 3 provides the design of APEFS. Section 4 presents the idea how to improve it. Section 5 describes related work, and Section 6 concludes the paper and points out directions for future work.

2   Android and Security

This section gives an overview about Android's permissions system and the software platform Google Play.

2.1   Permissions

In Android every app runs in a sandbox to prevent apps from performing operations that impact other apps, the operating system, or the user. As an example, an app can not make phone calls or send SMS by default, to prevent costs for the user.

To use features like calling persons, send SMS or use the internet connection, the app must declare permissions that it wants to use. These permissions are categorized in three threat levels: *Normal*, *Dangerous* and *Signature/System*. For a normal app developer only the first two are accessible, because Signature/System permissions are restricted to pre-installed apps.

In order to install an app, the user must accept all permissions that the app requests. There is no way to decline single permissions that a user doesn't want to grant.

Apps can also define their own permissions, for example to protect a content provider that should only be accessed by selected apps. In this article we focus on the permissions given by the Android system.

2.2 Google Play

Like the other mobile software platforms (e.g. Apple App Store, Windows Phone Marketplace), Android provides a centralized app platform where the users can search for, download, and install apps. Google Play [2] (former Android Market) contains about 450,000 apps[15] and supports charts in different categories sorted by free and charged apps.

After finding an app, the user must approve the presented permissions that the app requests, in order to install it. There is no way to decline single permissions.

By default, Google Play gives no option to filter for permissions, so the user first searches for apps that would fit his needs and then filters this list of apps manually for an app that fits his security level, or de facto installs apps without even noticing the permissions.

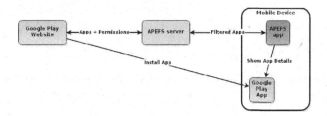

Fig. 1. Schematic of the APEFS-infrastructure

3   APEFS

We have developed APEFS, an infrastructure that gives a user the chance to filter apps by his own idea of what apps should be able to or not, without requiring root access to the device.

It consists of two components that use services provided by Google, on the one hand the Google Play Website and on the other hand the Google Play-App installed on the devices. On the device, there is the APEFS app, and in the back there is a database server. The schematic diagram of the infrastructure of APEFS is pictured in Fig. 1.

3.1   The APEFS-Server

The APEFS server has arisen from the wish to generate statistics about apps and permissions. We have therefore created an application that sends requests to the Google Play Website to get the chart websites for several different charts. Those websites can be parsed for package IDs. With these IDs we can access the detail websites for every single apps and parse them for information like developer name, price, rating, and especially the requested permissions. This information is saved in a database.

We used the database to create different statistics like Fig. 2 on the left which shows that most of the paid and free apps in the Top 500 request less than 10 permissions. Another statistic is shown in Fig. 2 on the right where one can see that free apps usually request more permissions than paid apps. We update the information every night, so our information is relatively up to date for statistics and we have the chance to watch movements in the charts. It is also possible to create statistics besides the Top 500, but then there is no direct reference to the popularity of the apps.

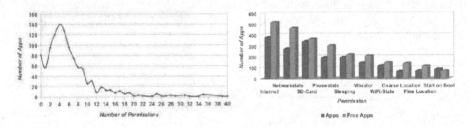

Fig. 2. Left: Total number of permissions used by the single Top 500 free and paid apps. Right: Top 10 used permissions by free apps vs. paid apps in the Top 500s.

Besides statistics, the APEFS server is a way for us to cache information from the Google Play website as seen in Fig. 1. This is important for the performance of the APEFS app, which will be described in the next section.

3.2   The APEFS App

The APEFS app is installed on the device. It gives the user the chance to use and create profiles, search and filter apps and then uses the pre-installed Google Play-App to install the apps.

Profiles: By default an app has no permissions in Android. Similar to that we build our filter app. So by default it filters all apps that want to have any permission. In order to let apps pass this filter, the user can use pre-defined profiles with certain permissions an app may have. For example, there are profiles for "only internet" or "camera and media access".

Advanced users may edit these pre-defined profiles or create their own ones. For non-advanced users, we added another abstraction layer to create own profiles, so that they need not go through the list of all 120 permissions that Android provides. The permissions are summarized to packages like "read personal data" for READ_CONTACTS, READ_CALENDAR, READ_SOCIAL_STREAM, READ_SMS and READ_HISTORY_BOOKMARKS.

Search and Charts: The APEFS app provides a search facility and the charts based on the localized Google Play website. Before searching, the user may activate different profiles to filter the search. To our knowledge there is no official API to read contents Google Play, so we created our own way by parsing the HTML-pages of the Google Play website. There was an unofficial API for Android Market but it doesn't work any more[1].

After the user has given a query, the APEFS app sends it to the APEFS server including the filters. The APEFS server sends the query to the localized Google Play website and parses the result for IDs. These IDs are the package names and should be unique. The APEFS server then searches for the IDs in its local database, which acts as a cache to keep performance, filters out the apps not fitting to the filters and sends the information about the resulting apps to the APEFS app. If the APEFS server doesn't find information about the app in its database, it sends a request for this app to the Google Play website and parses the resulting web page for the requested permissions. The same procedure is done for the charts of the individual categories.

In an early version of APEFS we didn't have a cache server and did all the parsing and caching on the device. After testing we decided to use an external cache server, because the performance was way to slow. This results from the local cache which is too small and so there is a high cache miss rate. The server has a bigger cache because it is used by many users at the same time and raises thereby the cache hit rate.

As with any cache server we have the problem that the cached information may become out-of-date, when an app is updated and the new version requests different permissions. We update the database every night, but that would not be sufficient, because if the information is outdated and the app now requests more permissions there would be a security leak because the user trusts in our app that it would filter the apps right. So we have to update after the user clicks on an app in the search result. Then we ask the Google Play website for the actual information about the app and inform the user if there has been a permission change so that the permissions don't fit the selected profiles any more. In this step we also update the database entry for the app so that future searches are more precise.

---

[1] http://code.google.com/p/android-market-api

Installation: We wanted APEFS to be usable without a need for root-access to the device or even requesting many permissions. Another goal was to use the original software platform given by the operating system, in this case Google Play. So the decision was to use the normal Google Play app to install the apps. This is possible by using an `Intent` that starts Google Play on an app identified by its package name, as shown in Listing 1.1. So the user is linked to this page and can then install the app with the normal mechanism. He is also able to read the comments and watch the screenshots here, because we have not showed them in the APEFS app so far.

Listing 1.1. Show app in Google Play App via Intent

```
String packageName = "com.test.app";
Uri appUri = Uri.parse("market://details?id=" + packageName);
Intent appIntent = new Intent(Intent.ACTION_VIEW, appUri);
startActivity(appIntent);
```

Installed Apps: Another feature provided by the APEFS app is that it can search the installed apps and show all apps that do not fit to the defined profiles. Thereby the user can detect default apps and apps he has installed before, which do not fit his security level and can delete them afterwards. The installed apps and their permissions can be accessed as shown in Listing 1.2, without requesting an additional permission.

Listing 1.2. Access installed apps and their permissions

```
PackageManager pm = getPackageManager();
List<PackageInfo> pis = pm.getInstalledPackages(PackageManager
    .GET_PERMISSIONS | PackageManager.GET_META_DATA);
for (PackageInfo pi : pis) {
    String packageName = pi.packageName;
    String[] permissions = pi.requestedPermissions;
    ...
```

4   App-analysis

APEFS as described in the last section gives the user the power to filter apps against user-defined permission profiles. By their nature, permissions only determine whether or not an app can *access* a certain piece of information. Once access is granted, there is no restriction anymore on how the app actually *uses* this information. However, users of handheld devices are most often concerned about exactly this use of private data. E.g., in principle there is no problem with an app accessing a user's contacts, as long as it does not post them to the internet. With a pure permission system, the only way to achieve this would be to either refuse the "contacts" permission or the "internet" permission, both of which could be impractical for certain apps. For instance, consider an app that should use the contact data for making phone calls or sending SMS and just needs the internet permission to display some advertisements.

Another problem is that, among others, the pictures and other contents of the external storages are not protected by the permission-system of Android at all.

Thus, permissions alone are insufficient by nature to ensure that an app respects a certain level of privacy. That this is indeed an important issue is proven by investigations of apps like, e.g., in [9], where out of 30 randomly selected popular apps, 15 leak location data to an advertisement server without requiring any user consent. To solve this problem, we need a way to determine possible flows of information in an android app, to filter apps based on a specification of allowed and disallowed information flows and, finally, a mechanism to ensure an app's conformance to this specification. Since we want to select apps based on their behavior before even installing them on the device, existing approaches like TaintDroid [9] are not sufficient, since they analyse the information flow only at run-time.

We decided to use a combination of static byte code analysis with assertions checked at run-time.

4.1   Information Flow Analysis

To get some knowledge about how an app actually uses certain sensitive data, we employ static information flow analysis [18], a special type of data flow analysis [1]. More ecactly, we determine whether information from a predefined set of sources can possibly flow to given output channels of the handheld device.

In order to start this analysis, the first step is to decompile the dex-file in the apk-package used in Android. For this purpose, we used the ded tool [17] created by Octeau et al. This tool recreates the class-files with normal Java bytecode from the compact dex-file with Dalvik bytecode. After that, the class-files can be analysed using normal Java bytecode analysis frameworks.

For the analysis we choose the Soot framework [20] because of its liveness and good support for interprocedural data flow analysis, including pointer analysis. To determine possible information flows in an app, we use the following forward flow analysis:

$$\text{in}(b) = \bigcup_{p \in \text{pred}(b)} \text{out}(p)$$

$$\text{out}(b) = \text{gen}(b) \setminus \text{kill}(b) \cup \bigcup_{v \in \text{in}(b)} \text{copy}(b, v)$$

where for each statement b in the app's intermediate representation

- $\text{in}(b)$ is the set of variables containing sensitive data at the beginning of b,
- $\text{out}(b)$ is the set of variables containing sensitive data at the end of b,
- $\text{pred}(b)$ is the set of possible predecessor statements of b,
- $\text{gen}(b)$ contains all variables that may be assigned with sensitive data by b,
- $\text{kill}(b)$ contains all variables that are definitely assigned with non-sensitive data by b,
- $\text{copy}(b, v)$ is the set of variables to which b may copy information from v.

Once this interprocedural flow problem has been solved, we scan the intermediate representation for a statement b which writes a variable $v \in in(b)$ to an output channel. If we find such a statement, the app may possibly leak sensitive information. Otherwise, the app is guaranteed to respect our privacy specifications.

A common problem of this kind of static data flow analysis is that it always is conservative. This may result in an unacceptable number of false positives, where the analysis detects a possible leak of sensitive information, although in reality, there is none. In order to avoid these false positives, we employ run-time assertions. We will provide a tool the developer can use after compiling his app, which tells him where the problematic information flows are. The developer then can use assertions to tell the tool that there actually will be no flow. This information may be wrong, but since the assertions will be checked at run-time, the app will be terminated, if the assertion is not fulfilled.

4.2   Connection to APEFS

To connect the information flow analysis to APEFS, the first and relatively easy step is to extend the profiles so that the user can define sensitive data and permissible information flows.

The second step is that we filter the apps in the market, such that only apps that comply to a selected profile will be presented for a download. The problem here is that we need access to the apk-package of the apps to perform the information flow analysis. For paid apps, there is no way for the APEFS server to get access to the package from the market. So there is either need for an alternative market where the APEFS server could directly access the packages, or the apps must specify their information flow properties in freely accessible metadata.

The own market is the technically easier solution, because we have direct access to each app that is listed in the market. The problem is that it would be another market that is not installed by default on the devices, so it would be difficult to achieve acceptance by both users and developers.

For the second solution, there are two technical issues. The first one is to find a proper way to publish the required metadata on the app's information flow. A promising approach is the use of application specific permissions declared in the app's manifest [3]. The second and bigger problem is that there is no guarantee that this metadata actually is correct. This problem may be solved either by some kind of digital signature scheme or by verifying the information flow data immediately after downloading the app. The latter would require to perform the information flow analysis outlined in Sect. 4.1 on the handheld device. The evaluation of the different approaches and their implementation are part of our current research.

5   Related Work

Security and privacy are urgently required features for smartphones, so therefore there is huge body of work on it, for an excellent overview about the current state of research and future directions see [8]. We want to focus on the most closely related work.

The closest work is Kirin[10], an alternate software installation framework where the user can define security rules the apps must match in order to be installed. The difference to APEFS is that it does not use the official market and only installs generated apk files. This would be a possible solution for the problem of connecting the information flow analysis to APEFS.

SCanDroid[12] provides automated application certification using WALA, a Java bytecode analysis framework with permissions as security types. This is based on the previous work by Chaudhuri[7] where he proposes a formal model for tracking flows in Android apps.

Androlyzer[4] is a web-based tool which gives a user reports about the privacy leaks and suspicious functions in several popular Android apps. Unfortunately there is no documentation about how the tool works and the Androlyzer-App that should analyse the users apps can't be found in Google Play.

As the source code of the apps is not always available and more importantly static analysis is to conservative there is need for dynamic analysis of running apps. TaintDroid[9] proposed by Enck et al. identifies apps sending privacy sensitive data to network servers by using dynamic taint analysis. It therefore first taints the data and rises an alert message when the tainted data leaves the phone. As a result it is limited to only inform about sent data and has no chance to avoid the sending. Another problem of TaintDroid is that it must be flashed with its own firmware to the device, which results in a problem of acceptance.

An approach to hide data without affecting functionality of apps is to give the apps fake data. There are several projects that use this technique, for example MockDroid[6] and TISSA[21]. MockDroid fakes location and phone identifiers and provides functionality to time out internet connections or return empty SMS, contact or calendar results. TISSA also fakes those information but is slightly more flexible, by letting the user choose whether empty, anonymized, or fake information should be used. Both use TaintDroid to evaluate their effectiveness.

AppFence[16] proposed by Hornyack et al. extends the usage of fake data with blocking network transmissions containing tainted information by using TaintDroid. The user can therefore specify information that may not leave the device. AppFence also uses unique phone identifiers for every app and phone.

On the topic of analysis of Android's permission system and its usage, Barrera et al.[5] performed a study of permission usage by apps with self-organizing maps. By using this technique it is possible to inspect the usage visually. One result of their work is that only a small subset of permissions is used very frequently, where a large subset is only used by very few apps.

Another study provided Teufl et al.[19] by analysing the Android Market with Activation Patterns. Activation Patterns transform raw data into patterns for different analyses like semantic search, feature relation and anomaly detection. Especially the anomaly detection can be used for malware detection.

6   Conclusion and Future Work

APEFS offers the power for a user to filter apps by their permissions, so a user can look for apps that fit his own level of security and privacy. By employing this infrastructure the usage of permissions is simplified and strengthened, because users are encouraged to think about security issues before selecting an app, rather than just accepting some terms and conditions after the fact, probably without even reading them.

The shown limitation of APEFS, that permissions do not really show how an app *uses* sensitive information will be eliminated by employing static inter-procedural information flow analysis of the apps to find out whether sensitive information flows to some output channels of the device. The implementation of this analysis, which must respect Android's app communication structure, its extension with run-time assertions to avoid false positives, and the integration in APEFS remain the challenges which will be addressed in our future research.

References

1. Aho, A.V., Lam, M.S., Sethi, R., Ullman, J.D.: Compilers: principles, techniques, and tools. Pearson/Addison Wesley (2007)
2. Android-Apps on Google Play, https://play.google.com/store/apps
3. Android Developer's Guide – Security and Permissions,
   http://developer.android.com/guide/topics/security/security.html
4. Androlyzer – Know more about your apps, http://www.androlyzer.com
5. Barrera, D., Kayacik, H.G., van Oorshot, P.C., Somayaji, A.: A Methodology for Empirical Analysis of Permission-Based Security Models and its Application to Android. In: Proceedings of the ACM Conference on Computer and Communications Security (2010)
6. Beresford, A.R., Rice, A., Skehin, N., Sohan, R.: MockDroid: Trading Privacy for Application Functionality on Smartphones. In: Proceedings of the 12th Workshop on Mobile Computing Systems and Applications, HotMobile (2011)
7. Chaudhuri, A.: Language-Based Security on Android. In: Proceedings of the ACM SIGPLAN Workshop on Programming Languages and Analysis for Security, PLAS (2009)
8. Enck, W.: Defending Users against Smartphone Apps: Techniques and Future Directions. In: Jajodia, S., Mazumdar, C. (eds.) ICISS 2011. LNCS, vol. 7093, pp. 49–70. Springer, Heidelberg (2011)
9. Enck, W., Gilbert, P., Chun, B.G., Cox, L.P., Jung, J., McDaniel, P., Sheth, A.N.: TaintDroid: An Information-Flow Tracking System for Realtime Privacy Monitoring on Smartphones. In: Proceedings of the 9th USENIX Symposium on Operating Systems Design and Implementation, OSDI (2010)
10. Enck, W., Ongtang, M., McDaniel, P.: On Lightweight Mobile Phone Application Certification. In: Proceedings of the 16th ACM Conference on Computer and Communications Security, CCS (2009)
11. Felt, A.P., Chin, E., Hanna, S., Song, D., Wagner, D.: Android Permissions Demystified. In: Proceedings of the ACM Conference on Computer and Communications Security, CCS (2011)

12. Fuchs, A.P., Chaudhuri, A., Foster, J.S.: ScanDroid: Automated Security Certification of Android Applications,
    http://www.cs.umd.edu/~avik/projects/scandroidascaa/paper.pdf (accessed March 14, 2012)

13. Gartner, Inc.: Gartner Says Worldwide Smartphone Sales Soared in Fourth Quarter of 2011 With 47 Percent Growth,
    http://www.gartner.com/it/page.jsp?id=1924314

14. Genaim, S., Spoto, F.: Information Flow Analysis for Java Bytecode. In: Cousot, R. (ed.) VMCAI 2005. LNCS, vol. 3385, pp. 346–362. Springer, Heidelberg (2005)

15. Google+ Post by Andy Rubin,
    https://plus.google.com/u/0/112599748506977857728/posts/Btey7rJBaLF

16. Hornyack, P., Han, S., Jung, J., Schechter, S., Wetherall, D.: These Aren't the Droids You're Looking For: Retrofitting Android to Protect Data from Imperious Applications. In: Proceedings of the ACM Conference on Computer and Communications Security, CCS (2011)

17. Octeau, D., Enck, W., McDaniel, P.: The ded Decompiler. Tech. Rep. NAS-TR-0140-2010, Network and Security Research Center, Department of Computer Science and Engineering, Pennsylvania State University, University Park, PA, USA (2010)

18. Smith, G.: Principles of secure information flow analysis. In: Christodorescu, M., Jha, S., Maughan, D., Song, D., Wang, C. (eds.) Malware Detection, pp. 291–307. Springer, Heidelberg (2007)

19. Teufl, P., Kraxberger, S., Orthacker, C., Lackner, G., Gissing, M., Marsalek, A., Leibetseder, J., Prevenhueber, O.: Android Market Analysis with Activation Patterns. In: Prasad, R., Farkas, K., Schmidt, A.U., Lioy, A., Russello, G., Luccio, F.L. (eds.) MobiSec 2011. LNICST, vol. 94, pp. 1–12. Springer, Heidelberg (2012)

20. Valle-Rai, R., Hendren, L., Sundaresan, V., Lam, P., Gagnon, E., Co, P.: Soot – a Java optimization framework. In: Proceedings of CASCON 1999 (1999)

21. Zhou, Y., Zhang, X., Jiang, X., Freeh, V.W.: Taming Information-Stealing Smartphone Applications (on Android). In: McCune, J.M., Balacheff, B., Perrig, A., Sadeghi, A.-R., Sasse, A., Beres, Y. (eds.) Trust 2011. LNCS, vol. 6740, pp. 93–107. Springer, Heidelberg (2011)

A Guidance Model
for Architecting Secure Mobile Applications

Widura Schwittek, André Diermann, and Stefan Eicker

paluno – The Ruhr Institute for Software Technology
University of Duisburg-Essen
Universitätsstr. 9, 45141 Essen, Germany
{widura.schwittek,andre.diermann,
stefan.eicker}@paluno.uni-due.de

Abstract. In addition to fast technological advances in the area of mobile devices and its broad adoption in todays developed societies, mobile applications do not only address the consumer electronics market but are also increasingly being used in a business and industry context. Thus, we see a demand for research developing software systems comprising mobile devices with special respect to security concerns. In this paper we want to address this demand from an architectural point of view and make use of the concept of architectural decisions. We present a guidance model that supports on the one hand this decision-making process during architecting mobile applications. On the other hand the presented guidance model serves as a tool to evaluate existing architectures. The guidance model has been created based on an adapted version of Zimmermann's SOAD framework, which is used for in the context of service-oriented architectures. The guidance model itself consists of a set of interrelated architectural decisions for recurring design situations. The application of the guidance model is demonstrated along a real-world scenario. The guidance model also takes into account that security concerns are changing and therefore provides an extension mechanism which is presented in this paper.

Keywords: guidance model, architectural decisions, architectural knowledge, security, mobility, mobile applications.

1   Introduction

Despite the many benefits developed societies are currently experiencing in a so called mobile world, where everyone is connected with each other using a mobile device, for many new risks doors are opened and threats and security concerns are raised. Ideally, these concerns should be addressed during the development time of a software system for such an environment [1,2,3].

In this paper we consider security as a quality-attribute of software-intensive systems determined by its architecture and constrained by a context – in this case the use of mobile devices. We also consider architecting as a decision-making process, where architectural decisions are treated as first-class citizen. This view is discussed in the software architecture community for some years now [4,5,6].

A.U. Schmidt et al. (Eds.): MOBISEC 2012, LNICST 107, pp. 12–23, 2012.

Our goal is to provide a guidance model that supports this decision-making process during architecting mobile applications with special respect to security concerns. For this guidance model we collected architectural decisions which help the software architect during recurring design situations to identify decisions to be made, but also to access knowledge about design alternatives. Another use case of the guidance model is to evaluate architectural designs already made for existing architectures. One way of doing this is to use the guidance model as a check list to ensure that all architectural security concerns have been completely considered.

We base our work on Zimmermann's approach [7] which considers architectural decisions not as a matter of fact, which should be documented after all choices have been made, but as reusable design assets. The assumption is, if architectural decisions are identified, abstracted, codified and presented correctly that they might become as valuable for software architects as other reusable design knowledge like design patterns [8].

This paper is structured as follows: In section 2, the specialties of architecting mobile applications with special respect to security concerns are described. We then present the structure of the guidance model in section 3, which is based on the structure of the guidance model for architecting service-oriented architectures (SOAs) [7]. We present the contents of the guidance model as well as the content creation process in section 4. A concrete application scenario taken from a development project of a mobile application for a German company is used to illustrate the application of the guidance model in section 5. In section 6, it is explained how the application of the guidance model can lead to extensions and how this is realized, whereas related work is described in section 7. Both, conclusions are drawn and an outlook for further research is given in section 8.

2   Security of Mobile Applications

What is the difference between developing mobile applications and developing applications that run on stationary computers? And what are the specific security issues that emerge when developing mobile applications? To give an answer to this questions the distinct characteristics of mobile applications are described in the following and examples of possible risks and threats which raise security concerns are given.

Typical characteristics of developing mobile applications can be made explicit by looking at the devices that run mobile applications: They are small and movable and therefore can easily get lost or stolen, which in turn might lead to losing control over sensitive data or access to private networks [9,10]. We speak of **location-independent** as one characteristic of mobile applications.

Mobile devices are also **constrained by resources**. Although steadily improving, they still lack of bandwidth and processing power compared to stationary computers. This aspect might therefore have an impact on decisions concerning the use of cryptographic methods for example. Another characteristic to keep in mind is the small display size of mobile devices which might lead to the use of weak password in the case of touch screens.

Furthermore, a multitude of possibilities to have a **connection** to a device – such as through the telephone network (GSM, EDGE, GPRS, UMTS) and other wireless networks (IEEE 802.11, near field communication (NFC), Bluetooth, infrared) – break the boundary of needing physical contact to access sensitive data. But even in situations where physical contact is required allows access to stored data through malfunctioning third party components. Possible attacks are breaking or circumventing password protections, exploiting flaws in the USB or Bluetooth driver stack or accessing an unencrypted hardware drive directly. Additionally, transmitting data in general – if wireless or not – can principally be spied upon. The many possibilities of being connected make it difficult for the user to retain control and stay informed about security issues in the involved software components. Retaining control is even more relevant considering the fact that connectivity to public networks means being exposed to millions of other humans.

A typical mobile application has a server-side counterpart, which stores data at a central point and can be accessed by everyone who is using the application on the mobile device. Mobile applications are connected to systems that rely mostly on the same technologies which are used for web applications. This means that they are at the same risk being sensitive for all known and yet unknown server software exploits. It can also be stated that security decisions do not only concern mobile applications but also back-end servers. A holistic view incorporating the server-side counterpart or other **connected systems** and devices is required when deciding upon security aspects.

While in private each individual is responsible for any misuse or possible loss of sensitive data, businesses promoting the mobility of their employees have even more valuable data at stake. The awareness for new security concerns resulting from new mobile technologies and changed usage behaviors has to be raised (**human factor** [11]).

As stated in [12,13,14], we also see security as a quality-attribute of software-intensive systems which are mainly determined by architectural decisions. This also means that the later a security issue appears during the software development lifecycle the higher the effort is to fix it and the more does it cost. Security concerns should therefore be treated seriously and as early as possible especially during the architecting phase. We see a strong demand in supporting the architect in doing so. On the one hand our aim is to raise the awareness of architects for security issues in the field of mobile applications; on the other hand we want to provide architectural knowledge in the form of reusable architectural design decisions in the field of mobile applications.

3   The Structure of the Guidance Model

The structure of our guidance model for architecting secure mobile applications is based on Zimmermann's structure for guidance models. During the last years, he worked on guidance models for a specific architectural style: service-oriented architectures (SOAs). The result is a vast repository of reusable architectural decisions which currently contains more than 500 decisions [15] and is still maintained and used in industry projects. The decisions were systematically identified using a method, which is part of his SOAD (SOA Decision Modeling) framework [7]. Although his guidance model aims at supporting the architecting process of SOAs, Zimmermann explicitly points out that "the use of guidance models as reusable assets also applies to other application genres" [8]. To reuse the structure of the guidance model within the domain of security and mobility some slight adaptations had to be made. In the following we present the structure of our guidance model and discuss the required adaptions.

SOAD is a generic framework for decision modeling and reuse. It also qualifies as a decision-centric software design method [7]. The essential element of SOAD is the SOAD meta-model, which describes all entities and their relations and serves as the formal underpinning for the guidance model. The meta-model is depicted in Fig. 1.

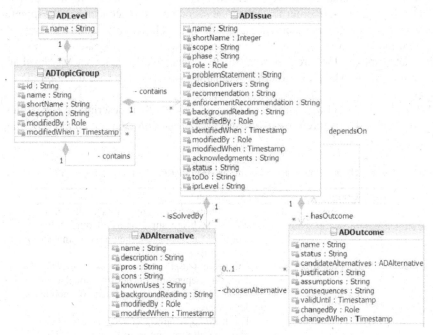

Fig. 1. The SOAD meta-model [4]

It contains the five entities *issue, alternative, outcome level and topic group.* The central entity is *issue* on which the architect has to decide upon, including a problem description and pointing to possible alternatives. An *alternative* corresponds to an optional solution for a particular design problem expressed through an *issue.* Finally, an *outcome* refers to an already made decision and its *justifications.* The entities *level* and *topic group* are used to structure all the issues (see Fig. 2). Zimmermann introduces four concrete *levels* (executive, conceptual, technology and vendor asset) and ten concrete *topic groups.* In this section, we focus on the entities *level, topic group, issue* and *alternative* as part of the considered guidance model. The concept of an *outcome* will be described in the next section, because it is only relevant for project specific decision models. Further information on the SOAD meta-model is provided in [7], [8] and [16].

Our detailed investigation of the model has shown that it can be fully applied to the domain of security and mobility. Therefore all entities, their attributes and relations were kept untouched. But adaptations were required to structure the issues using instances of the entities *level* and *topic group.* While all four levels are transferable, most of the ten topic groups are strongly related to SOA and can therefore not be used in our context. This leads to two questions: How can security concerns be organized into adequate topic groups and how do they integrate into the framework?

We have chosen the layer model for IT-Security by [17] to answer the first question. It differentiates security issues into five different layers. These layers proved to be suitable for structuring security related architectural decisions in the sense of SOAD's *topic groups*. In order to answer the second question concerning the integration, we replaced all SOA specific topic group by the IT-Security layers and arranged them into the level structure. The topic groups "infrastructure", "system", "communication" and "application" are used to refine the conceptual level, technology level and vendor asset level. The topic group "overarching aspects" only take place on the executive level.

Table 1 covers all newly introduced *topic groups* and their description. Fig. 2 illustrates our adapted structure for the guidance model including *levels*, *topic groups* and exemplary *issues*.

Table 1. Topic group derived from the BSI layer model for it security [17]

	Topic Group	Description
1	Overarching Aspects	This topic group comprises security decisions, which are superior to all other topic groups. That means that they have an impact on the other topic groups.
2	Infrastructure	The second topic group embraces security decisions depending on constructional conditions. In this context conditions of mobile devices are referred.
3	System	The third topic group covers security decisions on the system's level. Remote non-mobile systems (server) and mobile devices (client) are distinguished.
4	Communication	The forth topic group covers security decisions, which refer to communication. The focus is on data exchange between two or more systems. This contains different communication technologies as well.
5	Application	The fifth topic group contains security decisions on application level. These refer to aspects for the realization or operation of applications.

We analyzed further concepts that were either transferable directly to our context (e.g. dependencies between issues and alternatives in order to express logical or temporal relations) or were too SOA specific (e.g. the identifications rules or the meta-issue catalog techniques for identifying architectural decisions). Concerning the decisions identification process we instead combined a top-down and a bottom-up approach to identify relevant decisions. This is explained in more detail in section 4. As wrap up we can state, that it is indeed possible to transfer the concepts from the SOAD framework to the domain of security and mobility with slight adaptation effort.

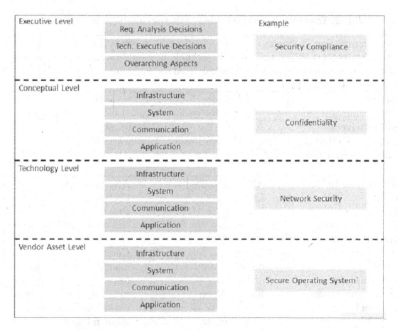

Fig. 2. Structure of the guidance model for security

4 Identification Process and Contents of the Guidance Model

Both, the process of populating the adapted structure with relevant decisions and the result are presented in this section. We followed the SOAD framework steps of *identifying*, *modeling* and *structuring* important security related architectural decisions. The other steps *tailoring*, *making* and *enforcement* will be described in the next section. As mentioned previously, we combined a top-down and a bottom-up approach to identify relevant decisions. The bottom-up approach is used to initially identify a set of decisions, which are then validated by the top-down approach. We advanced iteratively and incrementally within the bottom-up approach by conducting a literature survey [18,19,20,21,22]. The specialty of security is that it stays mostly invisible to stakeholders as long as no security issue is raised. So, when collecting architectural decisions on security we had to look at situations where systems might fail. Within the top-down approach, relevant decisions are identified by looking at security concerns and the characteristics of mobile applications discussed in section 2. The results are 35 unsorted and unordered decisions.

In a next step, we modeled the identified decisions using a template based on the SOAD meta-model. In Table 2, a template with the modeled issue "Transmission Technology" is presented. All template attributes further describe an issue on which to decide upon in terms of a name, problem description, literature, relations, decision drivers and alternatives. The attributes *scope*, *phase* and *role* are especially relevant for integrating the guidance model into a software engineering design method, as proposed by Zimmermann [7].

Table 2. Template showing modeled "Transmission Technology" issue

Name: Transmission Technology			Short Name: RAD17

Name: Transmission Technology   **Short Name:** RAD17
Problem Statement: Which transmission technology should be chosen from a security point of view and which impacts could be expected for the architecture?
Background Reading: [18]

Scope: communication, transmission	Phase: solution outline	Role: security engineer

Decision Drivers: importance of information, data load, performance, distance of communication points	Relations: influences RAD16

Alternatives:

Alternative 1: GSM **Pros:** First pan Europe mobile communication standard; widely spread **Cons:** low data rate; only one site authentication **Known Uses:** t-mobile network	Alternative 2: GPRS **Pros:** higher data rate by channel bundling **Cons:** no guarantee for end-to-end security **Known Uses:** watching WAP websites with "modern" mobile devices	Alternative 3: UMTS **Pros:** universal standard, higher data rate **Cons:** interoperability needed (downward compatibility), which enables man-in-the-middle attacks **Known Uses:** "current" mobile devices, surf-sticks
Alternative 4: WLAN **Pros:** high data rate **Cons:** wireless transmission (one-to-many communication) **Known Uses:** home networks	Alternative 5: Bluetooth **Pros:** Enables ad-hoc networks; coupling of devices ensures communication partner **Cons:** unregulated frequency band is fragile for interference disruptions; short distance (10 – 100m) **Known Uses:** head-sets	Alternative 6: NFC **Pros:** universal standard; specific short distance up to 10cm **Cons:** contact implies transaction affirmation, no dedicated precaution **Known Uses:** Mobile payment

Recommendations:
One selection driver is the local restriction of communication. WLAN, Bluetooth and NFC are designed for short distances with local restrictions, whereas GSM, GPRS and UMTS operate over large distances and could therefore be used location-independent. Another selection driver is the data load (e.g. WLAN features the highest capacity).

To assure a generic application of that model we do not constrain any of the attributes to a formal phase or role model. The attribute *scope* therefore refers to any element type within an architecture, which is affected by the decision. The attribute *phase* is related to its pendant given by a generic process model. Since architectural decisions will mostly take place in the design phase, we further differentiate this phase into the sub-phases solution outline, macro and micro design [7]. A common *role* within our guidance model is the security engineer, as an interdisciplinary expert with a sound knowledge in software architecture and security related topics [23].

Furthermore, we structure our identified decisions utilizing the levels and topic groups introduced in the previous section. The issues are classified according to their properties matching the level and topic group characteristics. This structure will help architects and stakeholders to get a faster and more efficient overview of the model. In Table 3 the result of that structuring process is presented.

Table 3. Security related architectural design issues for mobile applications

Level	Issues		
Executive Level	• Risks • Evaluation Criteria • Make or Buy • Open Source vs. Closed Source		• Security Strategies • Security Compliance • Policies
Conceptual Level	• Authenticity • Authentication • Integrity • Confidentiality • Availability • Non-Repudiation • Anonymity • Pseudonymity • Dependability • Trust • Security Models • Cryptography		• Access Control • Security Patterns • The Human Factor • Identity management • Security Principles • Sessions Management • Data Validation • Exception Handling, Auditing and Logging • Configuration • Multi-User Support • Patching and Updating • Physical Security
Technology Level	• Network Security • Transmission Technology		• Development and Application Technology
Vendor Asset Level	• Mobile Operating System		

Dependencies between elements can be described via relation types. One group of relation types indicate dependencies between issues (namely *influences*, *refinedBy* and *decomposedInto*). Another group of relation types indicate dependencies between alternatives (namely *forces*, *isIncompatibleWith* and *isCompatibleWith*). The last relation type called *triggers* is used to express temporal relations. All relation types are expressed through the relations attribute within the decision template (see relations attribute of the exemplary decision depicted in Table 2).

5   Applying the Guidance Model

In this section it is described how the security guidance model is utilized to implement a project specific decision model in which the identified issues from the guidance model are reused. The decision model has been derived from the architectural concept of a real development project for a German company. In this project a mobile application has been developed which served as a case study to validate the guidance model consisting of a set of architectural design decisions in the context of mobile applications. The project is situated in the banking sector and its objective is to make mobile devices applicable for employees in this sector by fulfilling particular security requirements. The main requirement was to ensure non-repudiability, which means, that every accomplished action is assignable and not deniable afterwards. Besides this, further requirements exist, e.g. to remotely control the mobile devices or enforce organizational policies on every mobile device. To guarantee a high degree of security for that mobility project, security measures are applied at architectural level, leading to security related architectural decisions. A project specific decisions model is created and used to make and enforce decisions for that project using our guidance model.

The first step of creating a decision model is to tailor the reusable guidance model by considering project specific properties. Two approaches are offered by SOAD [7]: the *tailoring technique* and the *decisions filtering concept*. We applied both approaches to our guidance model and identified 15 decisions which are relevant for the current use case. Most of them could be matched by their relations attribute. For example: every decision, which directly decomposes an already chosen decision, is also relevant for the current use case. There was also the need to modify some of the filtered decisions to fit project specifics, e.g. particular decisions drivers. After tailoring the guidance model, the decisions have actually to be made.

This is accomplished by following the activities *Managed Issue List* and *Decision Making Process* described in [7]. These activities support the software architect during decision-making. Making a decision actually means to choose an alternative within an issue and document the outcome with its justification. For example, after matching the given requirements and decision drivers for the previously filtered issue "Transmission technology", alternative 1 has been chosen to be used within the project (see Table 2). In Table 4 an excerpt of filtered issues, the chosen alternatives and their justifications is presented.

Last but not least, all choices have to be enforced. The decisions usually affect design models and development artifacts such as source code. To overcome the gap between our decision model and existing design models, a *decision injection* approach can be applied [7]. It follows the model-driven development concept, in which models are transformed and could then interact with design models. Due to the fact, that the industry project is still ongoing and our guidance model was used for conceptual coverage of the security aspect in this area, the enforcement step was not applied to the project.

Table 4. Excerpt of project specific decisions and their justification

Filtered Issue	Chosen Alternative	Justification
Authenticity	Knowledge	easy to implement, wide spread
Non-Repudiation	Auditing	given by project described in use case
Evaluation Criteria	ITSK	legal reasons
Secure Operating System	Android	high security and ability for customization
Authorization Standard	OAuth	implementation for that standard already exists

6   Extending the Guidance Model

By using our guidance model described in section 3 and tailoring a project specific decisions model based upon it, we gained additional security related architectural knowledge. Modeling architectural decisions seen as a knowledge management activity [24] leads to new knowledge which has to be codified as reusable asset within the guidance model. An iterative informal four-step bottom-up process exists to harvest gained architectural knowledge. This process is part of the SOAD framework and is used to enhance our guidance model. First, newly generated architectural knowledge in the form of architectural decisions gained from a completed project is taken as raw input. With the help of specific qualification criteria, decisions are integrated into the guidance model in a second step. The third step deals with hardening the captured decisions and the last step is to align the added decisions by fixing unappreciated or redundant dependencies.

The application of this process to our work shows, that first of all, most of the decisions from the guidance model could be employed. But as expected, it also turned out that additional decisions, which were previously not covered by the initial guidance model, have been made during the course of the architecting activity. For example, the project architect had to decide upon an *Authorization Standard* (see Table 4). This decision was not part of the initial guidance model and was later added during the tailoring step.

7   Related Work

When it comes to security knowledge within the field of software engineering, security patterns are often mentioned. Since patterns have a strong relationship to architectural design decisions [25], we want to point out that there exists a huge body of knowledge on security patterns like [21,26,27] and which are summed up here [28]. While security patterns mostly address design issues, design decisions go one step beyond by also capturing knowledge about vendor specific decisions which were identified in this paper and usually are not covered by patterns.

Our work is closely related to Zimmermann's decision repository [7] since we are using an adapted variant of his SOAD framework. The difference is the underlying architectural style, namely SOA. There are similar decisions to be found, but certainly not all, because of the focus on security and mobile applications in our work.

8   Conclusion and Future Work

In this paper, the authors presented a guidance model as a decision support instrument for security related architectural issues. It has been created based on an adapted variant of the SOAD framework. Both, the adaptions and the identification process are described in detail. Applying the guidance model in a real-world development project showed that the initial version of our guidance model already covered a broad set of relevant issues. Additional issues, which were not considered in the initial guidance model, could be harvested and integrated back resulting in a refined version of the guidance model.

During the architecting process in this industry project it turned out, that the guidance model enables a fast and simple reuse of architectural decisions. Especially the use of entry points and follow-up decision relations made it easy to create a decision model for secure mobile applications in a very short time. The guidance model also helped to increase the architect's awareness of basic security concerns to be considered during architecting, but also raised attention on aspects of security concerns that are special in the field of developing mobile applications. From this we conclude that the guidance model is also well fitted to be used as an evaluation instrument for software architectures (see also the concept of review checklists [8]).

Since this paper focused on security, we want to take further investigations on other quality attributes when architecting mobile applications in the future (e.g. energy consumption, performance and usability). Tools that manage all decisions and guide the architect within his favorite architecting tool are a desirable support. We also want to further investigate the links between our yet small repository of architectural design decisions on security of mobile applications and the SOA RADM repository used and hosted by Zimmermann and IBM.

Acknowledgment. This research was partially supported by the EU project Network of Excellence on Engineering Secure Future Internet Software Services and Systems (NESSoS, ICT-2009.1.4 Trustworthy ICT, Grant No. 256980).

References

1. Nekoo, A.H., Vakili, K.: A Practical Course on Mobile-Software Engineering: Mobile Solutions Laboratory. In: Conferene on Software Engineering Advances (2009)
2. Hu, W., Chen, T., Shi, Q., Lou, X.: Smartphone Software Development Course Design Based on Android. In: IEEE Computer and Information Technology, CIT (2010)
3. Rana O.F.: Software engineering for mobile environments. In: IEEE Seminar on Mobile Agents - Where Are They Going? (Ref. No. 2001/150) (2001)
4. Dannenberg, R.B.: Software architecture: The next step. In: Oquendo, F., Warboys, B.C., Morrison, R. (eds.) EWSA 2004. LNCS, vol. 3047, pp. 194–199. Springer, Heidelberg (2004)
5. Jansen, A., Bosch, J.: Software architecture as a set of architectural design decisions. In: Proceedings of the 5th IEEE/IFIP Working Conference on Software Architecture (WICSA), pp. 109–119. IEEE Computer Society (2005)
6. Van Der Ven, J., Jansen, A., Nijhuis, J., Bosch, J.: Design Decisions: The Bridge between Rationale and Architecture. In: Rationale Management in Software Engineering, pp. 329–348. Springer, Heidelberg (2006)

7. Zimmermann, O.: An Architectural Decision Modeling Framework for Service-Oriented Architecture Design. PhD Thesis, Univ. of Stuttgart (2009)
8. Zimmermann, O.: Architectural Decisions as Reusable Design Assets. IEEE Software 28(1), 64–69 (2011)
9. Masak, D.: Digitale Ökosysteme: Serviceorientierung bei dynamisch vernetzten Unternehmen. Springer, Heidelberg (2009)
10. Fuchß, T.: Mobile Computing - Grundlagen und Konzepte für mobile Anwendungen; mit 29 Aufgaben (2009)
11. Dwivedi, H., Clark, C., Thiel, D.V.: Mobile application security. McGraw-Hill, New York (2010)
12. Heyman, T., Scandariato, R., Joosen, W.: Security in Context: Analysis and Refinement of Software Architectures. In: Computer Software and Applications Conference, COMPSAC (2010)
13. Alkussayer, A., Allen, W.H.: A scenario-based framework for the security evaluation of software architecture. In: Computer Science and Information Technology, ICCSIT (2010)
14. Dai, L.: Security Variability Design and Analysis in an Aspect Oriented Software Architecture. In: Secure Software Integration and Reliability Improvement (2009)
15. Zimmermann, O.: Service-Oriented Analysis and Design a.k.a. SOA Decision Modeling, SOAD (2011), http://soadecisions.org/soad.htm
16. Zimmermann, O., Kopp, P., Pappe, S.: Industrial Case Study: Architectural Knowledge in an SOA Infrastructure Reference Architecture. In: Ali Babar, M., Dingsøyr, T., Lago, P., van Vliet, H. (eds.) Software Architecture Knowledge Management, pp. 217–241. Springer, Heidelberg (2009)
17. Bundesamt für Sicherheit in der Informationstechnik (BSI), IT-Grundschutz-Kataloge, https://www.bsi.bund.de/ContentBSI/grundschutz/kataloge/kataloge.html
18. Eckert C.: IT-Sicherheit. Oldenbourg-Verlag, München (2009)
19. Steel, C., Nagappan, R., Lai, R.: Core Security Patterns, 4th edn. Pearson Education (2009)
20. Viega, J., McGraw, G.: Building Secure Software. Addison-Wesley (2002)
21. Schuhmacher, M.: Security Engineering with Patterns. Springer, Heidelberg (2003)
22. Open Web Application Security Project (OWASP): Development Guide, https://www.owasp.org/index.php/OWASP_Guide_Project
23. Anderson, R.: Security Engineering. Wiley (2001)
24. Ali Babar, M., Dingsøyr, T., Lago, P., van Vliet, H. (eds.): Software Architecture Knowledge Management. Theory and Practice. Springer, Heidelberg (2009)
25. Zimmermann, O., Zdun, U., Gschwind, T., Leymann, F.: Combining Pattern Languages and Reusable Architectural Decision Models into a Comprehensive and Comprehensible Design Method. In: Seventh Working IEEE/IFIP Conference on Software Architecture (WICSA 2008), pp. 157–166 (2008)
26. Sorensen, K.E.: Session patterns. In: Pattern Languages of Programs Conference, PLoP (2002)
27. Weiss, M., Mouratidis, H.: Selecting security patterns that fulfill security requirements. In: Requirements Engineering Conference, RE (2008)
28. Yoder, J., Barcalow, J.: Architectural patterns for enabling application security. In: Pattern Languages of Programs Conference (1997)

Mobile Smart Card Reader
Using NFC-Enabled Smartphones

Frank Morgner[1,2], Dominik Oepen[1], Wolf Müller[1], and Jens-Peter Redlich[1]

[1] Humboldt-Universität zu Berlin, Institut für Informatik, Lehrstuhl für
Systemarchitektur, Unter den Linden 6, 10099 Berlin, Germany
{morgner,oepen,wolfm,jpr}@informatik.hu-berlin.de
[2] Bundesdruckerei GmbH, Oranienstraße 91, 10969 Berlin, Germany
Frank.Morgner@bundesdruckerei.de

Abstract. Due to the increasing use of electronic systems in all fields of
everyday life, users are now having to deal with electronic identification
and authentication practically every day. Password based authentication
systems are neither secure nor particularly convenient for users. Here, we
are presenting the idea of using an NFC-enabled mobile phone as a chip
card reader for contactless smart cards. A mobile phone can be used to
visualise, inspect and control electronic transactions. This mobile smart
card reader implementation enables ubiquitous, secure and convenient
two-factor authentication, the mobile phone being a very personal device
which users guard carefully and with which they are particularly familiar.
In this paper, we discuss the concept and implementation details of the
mobile reader and present a use case for the German electronic identity
card.

Keywords: two-factor authentication, mobile phones, mobile identity
management, USB CCID, skimming, trusted user interface.

1   Introduction

Simple authentication schemes use only one single factor to authenticate the
correct user: this can be a key that opens a door, a password to access an email
account or a signature on a remittance form, for example. Obviously, authentication is broken when the authenticator is stolen or compromised. An additional
authentication factor can mitigate this problem if the authenticators are kept
separate from each other. Nevertheless, two-factor authentication systems are
susceptible to active attacks [1]:

– Even if a service protects the user against phishing attacks, e.g. by introducing authenticators which are bound to a single session or transaction,
  a *man-in-the-middle attacker* (MITM) may still be able to mount a *relay*
  attack. For example, a fraudster could fake an online banking website to
  intercept a transaction, possibly modify this and then forward the modified
  transaction to the real bank. The attacker accesses the legitimate service using the authenticators provided by the user. This may be a simple password,
  a passphrase generated by a token or a signature on a smart card.

A.U. Schmidt et al. (Eds.): MOBISEC 2012, LNICST 107, pp. 24–37, 2012.
© Institute for Computer Sciences, Social Informatics and Telecommunications Engineering 2012

- With a *Trojan*, an attacker can read the user's input (e.g. passwords) and modify the displayed output (e.g. beneficiary of a credit transfer). Effectively, the Trojan is a MITM which has full control over the input and output of a user's computer. Even worse, the Trojan can also start transactions the computer's peripheral devices. A Trojan can, for instance, use a smart card for authentication when this is inserted into the reader. The legitimate user might only see an LED blinking on the reader—if he notices anything at all.
- We often need to use public terminals. ATMs or ticket machines can be manipulated (*skimming attack*). Similar to a Trojan attack, the attacker has full control over which actions are displayed to the user and which actions the terminal is actually carrying out.

Regardless of what authentication mechanism is actually used, many systems have one fundamental shortcoming—the lack of a trusted user interface [2].

Some chip card readers have a secure PIN pad. However, the reader's display is not often used as a secure output device. Even if it displays details of the transaction, the screen, typically very small, is not able to display all the necessary.In effect, the user will often not read all the information shown on the card reader's display. Furthermore, two-factor authentication using smart cards requires users to buy an additional device, which they would have to carry around with them permanently in order to be able to log in securely at any time. Even if users actually did this, they would not be able to use the smart card reader at public terminals, so this would not protect them against skimming attacks.

More and more new smartphones are being equipped with Near Field Communication (NFC) hardware. To a large extent, this wireless communications technology is compatible to the ISO 14443 series of standards for contactless smart cards, which means that smartphones can communicate with such cards.

In this paper we are presenting the concept of a *mobile smart card reader*: an NFC-enabled smartphone used as a chip card reader for contactless smart cards. Smartphones offer rich input and output options which would allow secure user authentication and transaction verification on the actual phone. When plugged into a computer, the phone is recognised as a standard smart card reader with its own PIN pad and display. We also describe a sample use case in which the mobile reader is used for authentication with the German electronic identity card.

1.1   Our Contributions

The main contributions of this paper are:

- to present and analyse the concept of a mobile chip card reader for two-factor user authentication;
- to present the use of the mobile reader as a trusted intermediary for defence techniques against relay attacks;
- to show partial implementation of the concept, including secure PIN entry functions based on PACE;
- to describe a use case of the mobile reader, namely with an identity card.

1.2   Structure of the Paper

In section 2, we give a brief introduction to the German electronic identity card (nPA). Here, we concentrate on those aspects and problems which also play a role for other smart cards. In section 3, we discuss the concept and implementation of the mobile smart card reader at greater depth. In section 4, we go on to present an informal security analysis of the concept and briefly discuss related work in section 5. Section 6 contains a summary of the paper and offers an outlook for possible future research.

2   German Electronic Identity Card

The German electronic identity card (nPA) is a contactless smart card conforming to ISO 14443. The chip has three applications, ePassport, eID and eSign. Although the chip's different applications are accessed in a similar manner, here we only need to discuss the eID application in more detail.[1]

The nPA's eID application can be used for electronic identification by e-Government or e-Business service providers (SPs). Since the eID application contains sensitive data about the card holder (e.g. name, address, date of birth), information is only revealed to authorised parties. Apart from this, the card holder can individually select or deselect what data are to be read, and finally authorise the transaction by entering his or her secret PIN.

The card holder can, for example, use his nPA to log into a website or state the delivery address for goods bought online. Accessing the eID application typically involves the following steps:

1. The card holder's web browser finds an object embedded in the SP's website, and this object starts a client application on the card holder's computer.
2. The client application displays the permissions requested by the SP and the purpose of the transaction (e.g. "login to the website").
3. The card holder checks the information and restricts the SP's permissions further if he wishes to do so.
4. The card holder authorises the transaction to the nPA by entering his PIN using Password Authenticated Connection Establishment (PACE).[2]
5. The SP and the nPA perform mutual authentication using terminal authentication (TA) and chip authentication (CA).[2]
6. The SP reads the data from the nPA using Secure Messaging (SM).

BSI TR-03119 [5] specifies three types of card readers for the nPA: A simple reader which only provides the ISO 14443 interface (Cat-B), a reader which must also feature a PIN pad (Cat-S) and finally the Cat-K reader which must additionally incorporate a display.[3]

---

[1] A complete overview is given in BSI TR-03127 [3].
[2] Cryptographic protocols to access the nPA (e.g. PACE, TA and CA) are dealt with in BSI TR-03110 [4].
[3] The classes also differ in security requirements and other functions which are not explained in detail here (see [5]).

With simple chip card readers which do not have a PIN pad, the user has to input his secret authenticator via the client application, where there is a danger that it might be stolen using malware. Furthermore, access to the smart card is not protected, so all applications on the card holder's computer can communicate with the card. This means that a Trojan can gain full control over the nPA whenever this is inserted in the reader and can then modify legitimate transactions and/or surreptitiously start new transactions.

Readers with a dedicated PIN pad protect the card holder's secret information from malware on the host computer, but the card holder may still be tricked into revealing the PIN by "social engineering". Also, a MITM[4] between the client application and the smart card reader might be able to modify a transaction on-the-fly, because communications with the reader are not protected. The user only sees the original transaction information on his computer screen and enters his PIN on the reader as requested—thus confirming the modified transaction.

To counter this kind of attack, the reader's display, which is assumed to be trustworthy, shows the transaction details. BSI TR-03119 requires the display to have at least two lines with 16 characters each which is typical for common smart card readers. This, however, does not give the card holder a complete and functional overview of the transaction. For example, the nPA offers a total of 15 independent permissions, which are shown in separate screens on the reader's display. Consequently, it is likely that the user will ignore the display and simply press "OK".

As far as the use of public terminals is concerned, the need for secure user input and output is an even more urgent issue. If, for instance, the card holder uses eID to prove his age in a video shop, he must allow the shop access to his card by entering his PIN. How can he be sure that the terminal does only what he is allowing it to do—and that it does not read more personal data from the card than has been permitted? In the past, it has been shown that skimming of credit card terminals can be performed at a low cost [2].

3   Mobile Smart Card Reader

The concept behind the mobile smart card reader is as follows: The smartphone is connected to a computer or public terminal and can then be used it as a secure input and output device for the smart card (see fig. 1). The mobile reader counteracts malware on the host computer and skimming at a public terminal. Although this concept is fairly straight forward, there are a number of stumbling blocks to overcome before it can actually be implemented. In this chapter, we shall address these problems. A more detailed discussion can be found in [6].

3.1   Standardised Drivers for Mobile Usage

Mobile connectivity is one of the great advantages of smartphones. Most devices offer multiple interfaces such as Wi-Fi, Bluetooth, USB or GSM/UMTS.

---

[4] The MITM can use malware either on the host computer or on a hardware module installed between the reader and the user's computer.

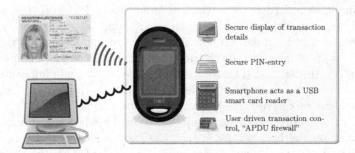

Fig. 1. Using the mobile smart card reader as secure input and output device for a computer that may not be trustworthy

Approaches for connecting the smartphone being used as smart card reader to a host computer could be just as diverse.

Even though wired connectors pose drawbacks—especially in mobile use cases—we advocate the use of USB for connecting the mobile card reader to the host computer, the reason being that USB is the only standardised method of communicating with smart card readers. USB CCID readers can be accessed on standard operating systems (including Windows, Mac OS and Linux) without any special configuration—currently-used operating systems usually come with the drivers installed.

Although USB CCID [7] specifications define some security related operations (e.g. PIN verification), the most recent Windows driver (2003 version) implements only simple commands for transmitting APDUs to the card.[5] This means that the PIN pad of an USB CCID compliant reader cannot be used without installing additional software (simple transmissions to the card are possible, however). On the other hand, the Unix driver libccid[6] is updated regularly and includes PIN pad support.

In order to use the mobile phone as a smart card reader, we have implemented an application called CCID emulator.[7] The emulator accesses the USB hardware through the Linux kernel module GadgetFS[8] (see fig. 2). Most USB chipsets on smartphones already support USB gadget mode to provide USB functionality to external computers (e.g. USB mass storage or USB networking). For smart card access on the mobile phone, we use OpenSC[9] which supports multiple interfaces—most prominently PC/SC—to communicate to the smart card.

---

[5] http://msdn.microsoft.com/en-us/windows/hardware/gg487509
[6] http://pcsclite.alioth.debian.org/ccid.html
[7] All software developed for this paper can be found at:
http://vsmartcard.sourceforge.net
[8] http://www.linux-usb.org/gadget/
[9] http://www.opensc-project.org/

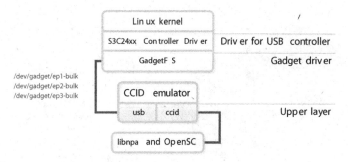

Fig. 2. Software layers of the CCID emulator running on the Openmoko Neo FreeRunner

3.2   Interface to Contactless Smart Cards

NFC is an umbrella technology encompassing such well-established standards as ISO/IEC 18092, the ISO/IEC 14443 series and JIS X6319-4. NFC supports three different modes of operation: peer-to-peer, card emulation and reader/writer. Interoperability of different NFC devices is one of the main focuses of the NFC Forum[10]. Mobile phones have limitations, e.g. with regard to chip complexity and power consumption. Consequently, the function range provided by NFC phones does not meet the needs of a dedicated smart card reader (e.g. regarding field strength or APDU size).

We expect the contactless chips of future phone's to provide the same functions as dedicated smart card readers. In the absence of fully compatible NFC-enabled phones, we chose to use an Openmoko mobile phone with an attached PN512 based board (extracted from Reiner SCT cyberJack RFID basis, see fig. 3). In this way we were able to avoid any problems which might arise from the differences between NFC and ISO 14443 and concentrate fully on the mobile reader concept.

3.3   Secure PIN Entry

In order to enter the PIN securely, the user must have a trusted interface to the intended application. This requires a trusted channel from the input devices to the application. To ensure that the user knows which application is requesting his authenticator and for what purpose, the application's output, too, must presented to the user in a secure form. User awareness is also greatly enhanced by the mobile smart card reader's consistent user interface—which remains the same even when it is used at different vendor's public terminals or points of sale.

The requirements of secure input and output will be discussed later (see section 4.1). On account of the mobile nature of the smart card reader presented here, it is desirable to use a PIN input method that reduces the risk of shoulder surfing (see section 4.2). Here, we shall focus on the technical aspects of communication between the host computer and the mobile smart card reader.

---

[10] http://www.nfc-forum.org

Fig. 3. Openmoko mobile phone with casing extension, PN512 board and antenna

Applications on the host computer communicate with smart card readers using PC/SC middleware. Smart card reader drivers map the PC/SC commands to the reader's hardware interface. For ease of implementation, USB CCID commands are very similar to their PC/SC counterpart. For example, the PIN verification data structure according to PC/SC pt. 10 [8] is almost identical to the PIN_VERIFY data structure in USB CCID so that the hardware driver only has to change the byte order where necessary.

The CCID emulator allows simple PIN verification and modification defined by USB CCID or PC/SC pt. 10, respectively. No modifications to existing drivers are required. These simple commands, however, are not suitable for the nPA, because the reader would send the PIN to the card via the contactless interface without any kind of protection. The CCID emulator therefore adds a new extension to USB CCID to apply the PACE key agreement protocol. This extension can be seamlessly integrated into the USB standard as it is equivalent to its PC/SC counterpart, in which PACE has recently been standardised [9].

Our solution for PACE via USB CCID requires modifications to existing drivers.[11] However, the traditional USB CCID and PC/SC commands do not have this restriction and can be used without leaving a footprint on the host computer.

3.4 Transaction Control and Visualisation

We want to empower the user to have greater control over what is exactly done with his smart card. Usually the user has to trust the transaction details shown on his computer screen, at a public terminal or on the point of sale device. With the mobile smart card reader, the user has full and precise control over all commands sent to the smart card.

The user can impose limits to the transactions he is willing to make with his card before the actual transaction even begins. During smart card communication, the reader passes on those commands to the card the user has allowed.

---

[11] The CCID emulator is provided with a patch for libccid.

Additionally the details are displayed to the user for confirmation. This might be called a "Man-in-the-Middle defence" [10]. The mobile smart card reader can also log all details of the transaction to obtain proof of what actions the user carried out and what actions he did not.

When the nPA is used for electronic identification, the first APDU from the SP commits itself to the permissions allowed in the ensuing transaction. In addition, descriptive data concerning details of the SP and the purpose of the transaction are transmitted to the reader. The CCID emulator displays all details *before* the user approves the transaction by entering his PIN.

When the SP sends APDUs to the nPA, the CCID emulator checks. One distinct advantage of the CCID emulator over existing smart card readers when handling an nPA is that it applies further sanity checks when the SP proves its authenticity using TA. For example, the CCID emulator checks the validity period of the SP's certificate against the current date. The CCID emulator performs all checks independent of the nPA. This additional mode of verification adds robustness to counteract potential smart card implementation errors.

It is important to design the user interface for the transaction inspection system so that it can be operated easily by most users. User interface design for security relevant programs running on an NFC-enabled phone is challenging due to a variety of factors such as space-constraints, environmental factors and the need to handle the card and the phone simultaneously. These problems are discussed in detail in [11].

3.5 Independent Smart Card Access

As a smartphone always comes with a battery, the mobile smart card reader is independent of a host computer. This allows the user to manage or inspect his smart card without having to rely on a computer or terminal. Depending on the actual type of smart card, the user can detect fraudulent transactions by reading data stored on the card. The user can also update any obsolete data stored on the card and change or unblock his PIN.

Independent PIN management can be used to create a *temporary PIN*. The temporary PIN does not reveal any details about the permanent secret information memorised by the user. This can be useful if the card has to be used on a terminal that does not support an external (mobile smart card) reader. When all transactions with the terminal are completed, the smartphone changes the PIN back to the user's permanent secret PIN.

The temporary PIN helps to reduce theft and tracking of the permanent secret PIN. However, one should keep in mind that the terminal has unhindered access to the card when the user inserts his card into the terminal and enters his temporary PIN. Usefulness of the temporary PIN and inspection or validation of data stored on the card depends on the specific type of card and should be considered individually for each case.

We developed a program for the nPA called `npa-tool`, which is based on OpenSC. It can change and unblock the PIN using PACE, thus enabling the user to enter temporary PINs for transactions at public terminals.

The `npa-tool` is also able to update the nPA's approximated current date, allowing the actual card to recognize when an SP is using an expired certificate. The card only updates its state if specially-crafted certificates are presented. A *date update service* as suggested in BSI TR-03127 [3] might be able to provide these certificates for the `npa-tool`. We have discussed other applications of the nPA combined with a mobile phone in an other paper [12].

4   Security Considerations

4.1   Secure Execution Environment

Many of the attacks that can be made on desktop systems can also be made on smartphones. Vulnerabilities of the software supplied with the smartphone, as well as third-party apps can impose a threat, even when installed from a trusted distribution platform.

User expectations and infrastructure of mobile phones and desktop computers differ considerably. Smartphones are expected to be reliable, whereas users of desktop computers are accustomed to errors. More importantly, most smartphone platforms are closed systems preventing access to hardware or core software. Most users knowingly accept these restrictions. This makes it possible to apply extensive security measures to the mobile platform.

Regardless of how a secure execution environment is specifically implemented on a smartphone, it should fulfil the following requirements [13]:

- protection of the software against external interference;
- observation of the computations and data of a program running within an isolated environment via controlled inter-process communication only;
- secure communication between programs running in independent execution environments; and
- provision of a trusted channel between an input/output device and a program running in an isolated environment.

A number of different isolation and verification techniques are suitable for mobile phones: Static and dynamic code verification [14], policy based isolation [15,16,17] or various types of virtualisation [18,19] possibly in combination with a hardware security module [20].

Correct implementation of software isolation is difficult. Again, the nature of the software distribution systems for mobile platforms can help to mitigate known problems. Critical software updates can be pushed to the smartphone by trusted parties—no user interaction is required. Also, a combination of security measures can be applied, for example, software verification *and* software isolation.

4.2   Protection against Shoulder Surfing

When a user enters a PIN on the mobile smart card reader in a public space, there is a danger that a potential attacker might see this. With the mobile smart card reader, the user can block the attacker's view by turning around in whichever direction he wishes, or by covering up the display.

His freedom of movement is limited only by the length of the USB cable. However, if a headset [21] or a pre-shared secret [22] is available, the user could also enter a modified version of the PIN which the attacker cannot use with the smart card alone. In addition, zero-knowledge proofs can be applied if the mobile smart card reader saves the PIN [23] securely.

4.3   Attacks via USB

Experience has shown that it is possible to compromise mobile phones and install malicious software via USB [24]. Therefore the USB connection to the host computer has to be regarded as part of the mobile reader's potential attack surface.

Mobile phones typically support several different USB profiles and their USB stack is generally more complex than that used with dedicated smart card readers, resulting in a comparatively larger the attack surface. A solution to this problem might be to introduce a dedicated smart card reader mode on the mobile phone. In this mode, the phone only supports CCID and all other USB drivers are unloaded from the kernel. This would reduce the attack surface of the mobile reader. Further research is required in this area.

5   Related Work

Use of an NFC-enabled mobile phone as an intermediary between the smart card and the terminal has been suggested in several publications. Two main use cases are under discussion in respective literature [25]: On the one hand a mobile phone may be used to carry out relay attacks [26,27]. On the other it may be used to inspect transactions and provide users with a trusted user interface [10].

Use of the nPA for two-factor-authentication on a mobile phone has also been suggested by Hühnlein et. al [28]. The authors suggest a security aware design for an Open eCard App to also provide defence against unconventional attack vectors. If possible, the Open eCard App should make use of platform-specific security features such as a Trusted Execution Environment. The Open eCard App should feature all the middleware aspects required by BSI TR-03112 [29]— including online communication to the SP. Vulnerabilities of the official client software for the nPA (AusweisApp) have shown, that this opens additional paths for conventional attacks. In contrast, our solution aims to reduce complexity by providing the reader interface only.

Mannan and Oorschot [30] propose a protocol called MP-Auth, which uses a personal handheld device (e.g. a mobile phone) to derive a one time password for authentication and session key agreement for use with an untrusted computer. The user has to enter, on his phone, both his long-term password and a nonce generated by the server. Furthermore, the server's public key must be stored on the phone, too. A one-time-password is then generated and the user has to enter this on the (untrusted) computer to authenticate himself to the server and establish a shared secret which is then used for the remaining session. The authors propose protocol steps for protecting the integrity of the nonce and transactions issued after the session has been established.

Hart et. al [31] propose using the SIM card in a mobile phone as a secure storage medium for web credentials. Their system uses either a browser extension on the client computer or a dedicated authentication server to request the (encrypted) credentials from the user's phone (via an SMS gateway). The browser extension approach is vulnerable to malware installed on the client computer, which can steal the user's credentials while they are being entered into the extension. Furthermore, the paper does not discuss the secure display of transaction information on the phone, so that in both approaches the system is vulnerable to phishing attacks.

Several publications have suggested to use the actual phone as an authentication token [32,33,34]. The main difference between these publications and this paper is that we do not propose to integrate the smart card into the mobile phone but use the phone as a trusted reader. This allows a solution which serves as a drop-in replacement for an existing infrastructure. Furthermore, keeping the smart card separate from the mobile reader makes our solution at least partially more robust against mobile malware because a compromised mobile phone does not have permanent access to the user's smart card.

A lot of research has been carried out regarding the security of various two-factor authentication schemes. For example, Drimer et al. [35] examined the CAP protocol used for online banking in Europe. Even though the protocol makes use of smart cards and trusted handheld readers, the authors found vulnerabilities in the protocols, which enabled them to perform a relay attack. This shows that even secure infrastructure cannot protect the user against failure at the protocol level. In contrast to proprietary protocols which rely on obscurity the protocols used for the nPA are freely available and have been proven to be cryptographically secure [36].

6   Conclusion and Future Work

In this paper we have discussed the idea of using an NFC-enabled mobile phone as a chip card reader for contactless smart cards. We have explained issues—implementation details as well as security considerations—that have to be taken into account when implementing a mobile smart card reader. We have discussed how the mobile reader can help to obtain secure user authentication in untrustworthy environments and how the mobile reader can be used as a trusted intermediary at a public terminal, which is susceptible to skimming attacks. Furthermore, we have described a use case for the German electronic identity card.

As discussed in section 4.1 a secure execution environment is of central importance for the work presented in this paper. A lot of research is currently being done on techniques for making mobile phones more secure, as well as on new attack vectors for these phones.

Our proposal centres around the use of NFC radio technology. This relatively new technology should be subjected to rigorous security evaluation, especially as it is being used in financial transaction systems such as Google Wallet.

Acknowledgements. Dominik Oepen is being sponsored by the German Research Foundation (DFG) Graduate School METRIK.

References

1. Schneier, B.: Two-factor authentication: too little, too late. Commun. ACM 48(4), 136 (2005)
2. Adida, B., Bond, M., Clulow, J., Lin, A., Murdoch, S., Anderson, R., Rivest, R.: Phish and Chips. In: Christianson, B., Crispo, B., Malcolm, J.A., Roe, M. (eds.) Security Protocols 2009. LNCS, vol. 5087, pp. 40–48. Springer, Heidelberg (2009)
3. Bundesamt für Sicherheit in der Informationstechnik. Technical Guideline TR-03127: Architecture electronic Identity Card and electronic Resident Permit, 1.13 edition (March 2011)
4. Bundesamt für Sicherheit in der Informationstechnik. Technical Guideline TR-03110: Advanced Security Mechanisms for Machine Readable Travel Documents, 2.05 edition (October 2010)
5. Bundesamt für Sicherheit in der Informationstechnik. Technische Richtlinie TR-03119: Anforderungen an Chipkartenleser mit nPA Unterstüzung, 1.2 edition (May 2011)
6. Morgner, F.: Mobiler Chipkartenleser für den neuen Personalausweis: Sicherheitsanalyse und Erweiterung des Systems nPA. Master's thesis, Humboldt-Universität zu Berlin (2012)
7. USB Implementers Forum. Universal Serial Bus. Device Class: Smart Card CCID (April 2005)
8. PC/SC Workgroup. Interoperability Specification for ICCs and Personal Computer Systems: Part 10 IFDs with Secure PIN Entry Capabilities, 2.02.08 edition (April 2010)
9. PC/SC Workgroup. Interoperability Specification for ICCs and Personal Computer Systems: Part 10 IFDs with Secure PIN Entry Capabilities – Amendment 1: PIN-Verification with Contactless Smart Cards based on PACE, 2.02.08 edition (2011)
10. Anderson, R., Bond, M.: The Man-in-the-Middle Defence. In: Christianson, B., Crispo, B., Malcolm, J.A., Roe, M. (eds.) Security Protocols 2009. LNCS, vol. 5087, pp. 153–156. Springer, Heidelberg (2009)
11. Oepen, D.: Authentisierung im mobilen Web: Zur Usability eID basierter Authentisierung auf einem NFC Handy. Master's thesis, Humboldt Universität Berlin (September 2010)
12. Morgner, F., Oepen, D., Müller, W., Redlich, J.-P.: Mobiler Leser für den neuen Personalausweis. In: Tagungsband zum 12. IT-Sicherheitskongress, pp. 227–240, Gau-Algesheim. SecuMedia Verlag (May 2011)
13. Gallery, E., Mitchell, C.J.: Trusted Mobile Platforms. In: Aldini, A., Gorrieri, R. (eds.) FOSAD 2007. LNCS, vol. 4677, pp. 282–323. Springer, Heidelberg (2007)
14. Bläsing, T., Schmidt, A.-D., Batyuk, L., Camtepe, S.A., Albayrak, S.: An Android Application Sandbox System for Suspicious Software Detection. In: 5th International Conference on Malicious and Unwanted Software (Malware 2010), Nancy, France (2010)

15. Nauman, M., Khan, S., Zhang, X., Seifert, J.-P.: Beyond Kernel-level Integrity Measurement: Enabling Remote Attestation for the Android Platform (2010)
16. Zhang, X., Acıiçmez, O., Seifert, J.-P.: Building Efficient Integrity Measurement and Attestation for Mobile Phone Platforms. In: Schmidt, A.U., Lian, S. (eds.) MobiSec 2009. LNICST, vol. 17, pp. 71–82. Springer, Heidelberg (2009)
17. Aciicmez, O., Latifi, A., Seifert, J.-P., Zhang, X.: A Trusted Mobile Phone Prototype. In: Proceedings of IEEE Consumer Communications and Networking Conference (CCNC 2008), Las Vegas. Samsung Electron. R&D Center, San Jose (2008)
18. Selhorst, M., Stüble, C., Feldmann, F., Gnaida, U.: Towards a Trusted Mobile Desktop. In: Acquisti, A., Smith, S.W., Sadeghi, A.-R. (eds.) TRUST 2010. LNCS, vol. 6101, pp. 78–94. Springer, Heidelberg (2010)
19. Hwang, J.-Y., Suh, S.-B., Heo, S.-K., Park, C.-J., Ryu, J.-M., Park, S.-Y., Kim, C.-R.: Xen on ARM: System Virtualization Using Xen Hypervisor for ARM-Based Secure Mobile Phones. In: Proceedings of IEEE Consumer Communications and Networking Conference (CCNC 2008), Las Vegas. Samsung Electron. R&D Center, San Jose (2008)
20. Kostiainen, K., Reshetova, E., Ekberg, J.-E., Asokan, N.: Old, New, Borrowed, Blue – A Perspective on the Evolution of Mobile Platform Security Architectures. In: Sandhu, R.S., Bertino, E. (eds.) CODASPY, pp. 13–23. ACM (2011)
21. Perkovi, T., Cagalj, M., Saxena, N.: Shoulder-Surfing Safe Login in a Partially Observable Attacker Model. Technical report (2011)
22. Hopper, N.J., Blum, M.: A Secure Human-Computer Authentication Scheme. Technical report, Carnegie Mellon University, Pittsburgh (May 2000)
23. Roth, V., Richter, K., Freidinger, R.: A PIN-Entry Method Resilient Against Shoulder Surfing. Technical report (2004)
24. Wang, Z., Stavrou, A.: Exploiting Smart-Phone USB Connectivity for Fun and Profit. In: Proceedings of the 26th Annual Computer Security Applications Conference, ACSAC 2010, pp. 357–366. ACM, New York (2010)
25. Anderson, R.: Position Statement in RFID S&P Panel: RFID and the Middleman. In: Dietrich, S., Dhamija, R. (eds.) FC 2007 and USEC 2007. LNCS, vol. 4886, pp. 46–49. Springer, Heidelberg (2007)
26. Francis, L., Hancke, G., Mayes, K., Markantonakis, K.: Practical NFC Peer-to-Peer Relay Attack Using Mobile Phones. In: Ors Yalcin, S.B. (ed.) RFIDSec 2010. LNCS, vol. 6370, pp. 35–49. Springer, Heidelberg (2010)
27. Francis, L., Hancke, G., Mayes, K., Markantonakis, K.: Practical Relay Attack on Contactless Transactions by Using NFC Mobile Phones. Cryptology ePrint Archive, Report 2011/618 (2011), http://eprint.iacr.org/
28. Hühnlein, D., Petrautzki, D., Schmölz, J., Wich, T., Horsch, M., Wieland, T., Eichholz, J., Wiesmaier, A., Braun, J., Feldmann, F., Potzernheim, S., Schwenk, J., Kahlo, C., Kühne, A., Veit, H.: On the design and implementation of the Open eCard App. In: GI SICHERHEIT 2012 Sicherheit – Schutz und Zuverlässigkeit (March 2012)
29. Bundesamt für Sicherheit in der Informationstechnik. Technical Guideline TR-03112: eCard-API-Framework, 1.1.1 edition
30. Mannan, M., van Oorschot, P.C.: Using a Personal Device to Strengthen Password Authentication from an Untrusted Computer. In: Dietrich, S., Dhamija, R. (eds.) FC 2007 and USEC 2007. LNCS, vol. 4886, pp. 88–103. Springer, Heidelberg (2007)
31. Hart, J., Markantonakis, K., Mayes, K.: Website Credential Storage and Two-Factor Web Authentication with a Java SIM. In: Samarati, P., Tunstall, M., Posegga, J., Markantonakis, K., Sauveron, D. (eds.) WISTP 2010. LNCS, vol. 6033, pp. 229–236. Springer, Heidelberg (2010)

32. Balfanz, D., Felten, E.W.: Hand-Held Computers Can Be Better Smart Cards. In: Proceedings of the 8th USENIX Security Symposium, Washington, D.C, pp. 15–24 (August 1999)
33. Hallsteinsen, S., Jorstad, I., Van Thanh, D.: Using the mobile phone as a security token for unified authentication. In: Proceedings of the Second International Conference on Systems and Networks Communications, ICSNC 2007, pp. 68–74. IEEE Computer Society, Washington, DC (2007)
34. Tamrakar, S., Ekberg, J.-E., Laitinen, P., Asokan, N., Aura, T.: Can Hand-Held Computers Still Be Better Smart Cards? In: Chen, L., Yung, M. (eds.) INTRUST 2010. LNCS, vol. 6802, pp. 200–218. Springer, Heidelberg (2011)
35. Drimer, S., Murdoch, S.J., Anderson, R.: Optimised to Fail: Card Readers for Online Banking. In: Dingledine, R., Golle, P. (eds.) FC 2009. LNCS, vol. 5628, pp. 184–200. Springer, Heidelberg (2009)
36. Bender, J., Fischlin, M., Kügler, D.: Security Analysis of the PACE Key-Agreement Protocol. In: Samarati, P., Yung, M., Martinelli, F., Ardagna, C.A. (eds.) ISC 2009. LNCS, vol. 5735, pp. 33–48. Springer, Heidelberg (2009)

Claim-Based versus Network-Based Identity Management: A Hybrid Approach

Faysal Boukayoua[1], Jan Vossaert[1], Bart De Decker[2], and Vincent Naessens[1]

[1] Katholieke Hogeschool Sint-Lieven, Department of Industrial Engineering,
Gebroeders Desmetstraat 1, 9000 Ghent, Belgium
`firstname.lastname@kahosl.be`
[2] Katholieke Universiteit Leuven, Department of Computer Science,
Celestijnenlaan 200A, 3001 Heverlee, Belgium
`firstname.lastname@cs.kuleuven.be`

Abstract. This paper proposes a hybrid approach that combines claim-based and network-based identity management. Partly by virtue of the principle of *separation of concerns*, better security and privacy properties are attained. Overall trust is diminished, while simultaneously reducing multiple actors' exposure and value as a target of attack. The proposed architecture also facilitates interoperability and pluralism of credential technologies, authentication protocols and operators. In addition, the user has more control over his personal data than with current network-based identity management systems. A prototype demonstrates the feasibility of the proposed approach.

Keywords: privacy, security, claim-based identity management, network-based identity management.

1 Introduction

Several definitions exist for identity management. The term is defined as follows by [2]: *Identity management consists of the processes and all underlying technologies for the creation, management, and usage of digital identities.* In practice, identity management involves the creation, maintenance, usage and destruction of an entity's identity, typically as an enabler to meet the needs of security and business applications [2,20].

Different taxonomies on identity management systems have been devised in the past [4,18]. The relevant distinction for this paper is between network-based systems and their more user-centric, claim-based counterparts [2]. Both comprise three major actors: the user, the service provider and the identity provider. In a network-based system, the user is typically redirected to an identity provider, which authenticates the user and supplies a *token* upon successful authentication. This token is then verified by the service provider and access is granted if it is valid. The procedure also includes the provisioning of any required user attributes, from the identity provider to the service provider. In a claim-based system, on the other hand, the service provider informs the user about the prerequisites to fulfill. If the user consents, he returns a *claim*. The latter can be

A.U. Schmidt et al. (Eds.): MOBISEC 2012, LNICST 107, pp. 38–50, 2012.

regarded as a response to the server's challenge, along with a verifiable statement about required user attributes. A claim may be endorsed by one or multiple issuers. The user sits in between the identity providers and the service provider, thereby controlling the information exchange between the two sides. This leads to less trust assumptions and better privacy properties in comparison to a typical network-based system, where the identity provider's role is more pervasive. The latter is also capable transaction monitoring and linking, collusion with other identity or service providers, and user impersonation. In addition, the concentration of multiple security-critical responsibilities makes network-based identity providers a high-value (single) point of attack. However, in terms of interoperability and standardisation, network-based systems have an advantage over their claim-based counterparts. For instance, deployment of eID technology is typically country-wide, thereby imposing additional efforts at best, or excluding international users altogether. Moreover, there is a need to facilitate the adoption of new privacy-friendly credential technologies [10,7,6,22]. The reuse of existing infrastructure and expertise is important in this respect.

Contribution: This paper synthesises a hybrid counterpart of network-based and claim-based identity management architectures, striving to leverage strengths and mitigate weaknesses. The modifications result in a clear separation of concerns, which yields advantages in terms of trust, privacy, security and interoperability. The feasibility of the proposed approach is demonstrated by a Shibboleth-based implementation that incorporates Idemix and the claim-based research architecture described in [22].

After elaborating on related work in section 2, an architecture is defined in 3. The latter is then validated in section 4, by means of the implementation and evaluation of a prototype. The section also explores possible extensions and variants. Following an overall evaluation in 5, conclusions are drawn in 6.

2   Related Work

The current identity management landscape is a diverse one. Among claim-based systems, we categorise data-minimising credential technologies (Idemix [10] and U-Prove [7]), government-deployed eID technology (e.g. the Belgian [12] and the German [6] eID) as well as conventional, X509 software certificates. The architecture described in [22] is claim-based as well. A number of claim-based systems offer interesting privacy and security properties. The German eID, for instance, requires a PIN entry before releasing personal attributes [5]. Moreover, it can generate service provider-specific transaction pseudonyms. Idemix and U-Prove, on the other hand, both provide pseudonymous and anonymous authentication and minimal attribute disclosure.

Popular network-based identity management systems include Shibboleth [17], which is widely used in educational institutions. OpenID [19] on the other hand, is used as an alternative to conventional username-password Web authentication. Proprietary infrastructures like Google's and Facebook's can also be listed here. The adoption of *purely* network-based systems is less hampered by the requirement for additional installations or configurations on the user's system, like many claim-based systems. Standardised specifications like SAML and ID-WSF are adopted and backed on an interorganisational level. Shibboleth, for instance, is used by major academic and research networks [24] [23].

Albeit each to its own extent, network-based systems have drawbacks. OpenID poses a wide range of security and privacy issues [8]. Moreover it lacks a mechanism for trust establishment (cf. Shibboleth federations). Network-based systems regularly have no support for selective attribute disclosure, although there are examples of the opposite. The concept is denoted as *permission-based attribute sharing* in the ID-WSF specification [3]. uApprove [14] is a plugin that enhances Shibboleth with similar functionality. These features and improvements contribute to privacy, compared to systems where they are not available. However network-based identity providers still have considerable power for transaction linking and monitoring, profiling, collusion with other identity providers or service providers. Lastly, they combine storage of user information and user authentication, 2 security-critical tasks.

Related research has been put forward by Dodson et al. [13]. It proposes a phone-based out-of-band authentication to an OpenID provider using a symmetric key-based challenge-response protocol. The approach by [15] is similar, combining the German eID with OpenID. Apart from hindering phishing, both approaches also replace user names and passwords by strong authentication. However, the OpenID trust establishment issue remains unsolved. Moreover, as the OpenID provider still stores user attributes, it remains a high value attack target. The approach by Leicher et al. [16], on the other hand, integrates the infrastructure of a user's mobile phone operator into OpenID. Besides the improvements of the two previous works, this approach also introduces trust establishment in OpenID by relying on trust in the operator and on the tamperproofness of a SIM card. Furthermore, it extends OpenID pseudonymity and anonymity. However, it mainly focuses on attaining better security, privacy and usability. Interchangeability of claim-based credential technologies and network-based authentication protocols fall beyond the scope of all three papers.

Additional related work is outlined in ABC4Trust [9]. It elaborates, among others, on how to integrate claim-based *Privacy-ABCs* in existing network-based systems. Their architectural margin for extensions is explored, after which integration strategies are discussed. However, each network-based system is treated separately. This paper strives to generalise this to support many claim-based technologies and network-based protocols, leaving the eventual choice up to the user's preference.

3   Architecture

In this section, the architectural requirements are introduced. Subsequently, we discuss modifications to network-based systems to satisfy these requirements.

3.1 Requirements

General Requirements

G_1 Security issues in the network-based authentication protocol, are resolved or mitigated. The specific problems and the extent to which they are treated, is specific to the network-based system that is considered.

G_2 Pluralism of operators, claim-based credential technologies, as well as network-based authentication protocols, is facilitated [11].

User Requirements

U_1 User trust in the network-based identity provider is decreased. Depending on the incorporated claim-based and network-based systems, this requirement ideally results in reduced capabilities for transaction linking and profiling.

U_2 The user has control over which personal attributes are released.

U_3 Switching to a different claim-based technology, poses no inconvenience to the user.
It is technologically easy for the user to switch to a another claim-based credential technology.

Service Provider Requirements

SP_1 Service providers can obtain reliable user information for service personalisation.

SP_2 The service provider is agnostic towards credential technologies and authentication protocols: he needs to support only few implementations to reach the majority of users.

3.2 Components

The proposed architecture is depicted in figure 1. There are four components: the *service provider*, the *identity broker*, the *user agent* and the *claim provider*.

Service Provider. Service providers offer personalised services to users. To enable personalisation, the release of a set of user attributes is required during authentication. Service providers interact with an identity broker (see below) to authenticate users and obtain personal information from them. Hence, their role and implementation is unchanged, compared to the original network-based service providers.

Identity Broker. Similar to claim-based systems, the user presents to the identity broker a claim proving the fulfillment of the service provider's requirements. However, in the proposed architecture, the identity broker extracts the user attributes or their properties, and provisions them to the service provider. This is performed according to a the network-based authentication protocol. Hence, brokers can be regarded as a conversion layer. They no longer store and maintain user information.

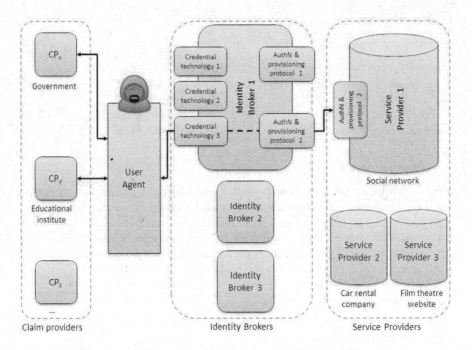

Fig. 1. The proposed identity management architecture

An identity broker implements credential-specific connectors to authenticate the user and obtain required user attributes. Each connector supports a credential technology. Once proven, the required attributes are transferred to service provider. This step can be achieved using any network-based authentication protocol that is supported by the identity broker: OpenID, SAML,...

Claim Provider. The claim-based identity provider, or claim provider for short, corresponds with the issuer of a claim-based system. It is henceforth the only responsible for user attribute storage and maintenance, whereas the network-based identity provider is transformed to an identity broker. Each claim provider can support a different technology.

User Agent. Similar to the ABC4Trust project terminology, the user agent is responsible for managing the user's claims. Multiple technologies may be incorporated. Some necessitate no online presence of the claim provider during authentication, while others may require the user agent to fetch additional credentials or attributes on the fly. This component is typically implemented on a (portable) device, like a smartphone or a smartcard.

Apart from managing credentials and authenticating the user to service providers, the user agent also implements other useful functionality [21]. This may include a connection component, providing support for different communication types: TCP/IP-based socket connections, HTTP, Bluetooth, etc.

Furthermore, a privacy component can display the service provider the user is authenticating to, along with the personal attributes that are about to be released. In addition, the user agent allows the user to select the claims he wants to authenticate with. User preferences can be automated as policies. They comprise restrictions that can be posed on communication channels, credentials, attribute disclosure,... Lastly, the user agent can also give feedback about the anonymity impact of the ongoing authentication.

3.3   Trust Relationships

This subsection shortly reflects on the changes in trust relationships.

User → identity broker: The identity broker attests the user's identity to the service provider. The user no longer needs to entrust the broker with the storage of his personal data, as this is now assigned to claim providers, of which the corresponding credential technology often provides better privacy properties purely network-based approaches. For instance, user profiling is far less trivial in an anonymous transaction where only a common attribute (e.g. *gender = "F"*) or a property thereof (e.g. *age > 18*) needs to be attested.

User → Claim Provider: The user trusts the claim provider to securely store a justifiable subset of his personal data. Note that, the user has multiple partial identities that are distributedly stored across claim providers. Additionally, this actor is also trusted to only perform authenticated provisioning to the user agent. The claim provider cannot monitor or link the user's transactions.

Service provider → claim provider: The service provider trusts the claim provider to only enforce genuine user attributes.

Service Provider → Identity Broker: The service provider trusts the identity broker to only assert verified attributes. Furthermore, the service provider may request from the identity broker to only accept credentials from a *trusted set of claim providers*. This allows the service provider to maintain a clear overview of trusted actors in the system.

4   Validation

A proof of concept of the architecture in section 3 is implemented using Shibboleth as a network-based identity management system. The Shibboleth service provider remains unchanged upon its integration in the proposed architecture. This implies that the network-based authentication protocol between the service provider and the identity broker is unaltered, compared to a standard Shibboleth configuration. The user agent is implemented on a smartphone for two major reasons. The device is nearly always in the user's presence *and* most often bound to the user exclusively. An additional advantage is the widespread adoption of smartphones. The user agent interacts with the identity broker. Modifications to Shibboleth to support this, consist of integrating authentication and provisioning support for the two claim-based credential technologies. The first claim provider is an Idemix issuer, whereas the second one is part of the identity management architecture described in [22]. Both systems allow for selective disclosure and support pseudonymous and anonymous transactions.

4.1   Interactions

Two distinct setups are implemented. In the first one, a service is consumed on the user's smartphone. In the second configuration, the Web service is accessed on a device other than the user agent (e.g. a workstation and a smartphone, respectively).

In both cases, the user's browser is typically redirected to the Shibboleth Discovery Service. Next, the user selects his preferred identity broker. The latter is responsible for the endorsement of the user's attributes. The next steps are discussed separately, due to the differences between both scenarios.

First Setup: The Device on Which the Service Is Consumed, also Contains the User Agent. In the first setup, the user agent on the smartphone has direct access to the session context of the transaction that was initiated with the identity broker. The user agent can, hence, authenticate the user through this session. This is similar to a standard Shibboleth setup that implements advanced authentication mechanisms, such as PKI-based authentication.

Second Setup: The Device on Which the Service Is Consumed, Does not Contain the User Agent. This is a more complex setup, as the authentication and the service request do not share the same session context. Therefore, a binding needs to be established between the two. This is carried out as follows:

1. the identity broker generates a QR barcode, containing a credential-specific authentication challenge. In addition, it also contains a policy that must be met for the authentication to succeed. For example, a policy may demand a proof that the user is over the age of 18, and that the authentication response be sent back only over HTTP. The barcode also contains the ID of the session that is to be authenticated.
2. the barcode is displayed by the device on which the service is consumed (e.g. a workstation). The user subsequently scans the QR code with his the smartphone.
3. the user agent generates an authentication response and transfers it back to the identity broker, using a secure and authentic out-of-band communication channel.
4. The authentication response is verified. If valid, the identity broker extracts the user's personal attributes (or properties thereof) from the response and generates a SAML response, which is subsequently transferred to the service provider, using the standard Shibboleth protocol.

4.2 Implementation Details.

The prototype builds upon Shibboleth v2. The last paragraph of section 3.3 mentions the ability of the service provider to specify a trusted list of claim providers. The implementation at hand, attains this by incorporating this list in the Shibboleth SAML Metadata. The latter is exchanged when service providers and identity providers join a Shibboleth trust federation.

Furthermore, the user agent is implemented on an Android-powered smartphone, running Idemix 2.3 and the identity management architecture in [22].

Authentication. Support for the two incorporated claim-based credential systems is added by implementing a *Shibboleth LoginHandler* for each credential technology. This component authenticates the user, also obtaining required personal attributes along the way. During this procedure, the identity broker transfers information about the service provider to the user agent. This allows the latter to inform the user about the authentication details.

Attribute Provisioning. The *standard Shibboleth approach* to impose restrictions on attribute disclosure, consists of the identity provider configuring *attribute filter policies*. Therefore, decisions about the disclosure of personal information are taken by the identity provider on behalf of the user.

The *proposed approach* entrusts the user with the decision of which attributes to disclose. The introduction of this notion, renders Shibboleth Attribute Filter Policies obsolete and leads to a new question. Namely, how can the user be informed of the service provider's policy? The prototype stores this policy in the Shibboleth Metadata, similarly to the trusted set of trusted providers. This allows the identity broker to obtain user attributes on behalf of the service provider.

Secure Credential Storage. Secure credential storage is implemented on the Giesecke & Devrient Mobile Security Card 1.0 [1]. The storage requirements differ, depending on the credential technology being used. The architecture in [22], for instance, relies on the tamperproofness of the card. Idemix however, can either be run entirely on the smartphone if speed is an important factor or with the master secret securely stored in the secure micro SD card.

5 Evaluation

This section evaluates to which extent the requirements from section 3.1 are fulfilled. A number of details and observations are discussed in 5.2. Paragraph 5.3 compares the merits and drawbacks of the proposed architecture to the two types of identity management it is inspired on. Finally, possible extensions are presented in 5.4.

5.1 Requirements Review

The identity broker is only responsible for user authentication and attribute provisioning. Storage of users' personal data is moved towards the claim providers, thereby reducing the identity broker's value and exposure as a target of attack. Additionally, some claim providers do not have to be online permanently, by which their issuance key is less susceptible to attack. Moreover, phishing attacks are less likely to be successful, due to the authentication feedback that is displayed by the user manager, in addition to the possibility to preconfigure the preferred identity broker on the user manager (see second paragraph of section 5.4). Therefore, the architecture positively contributes to requirement G1.

Since users are no longer bound to the same party for personal data storage on one hand and authentication and attribute provisioning on the other, they can more easily switch identity brokers. The latter are now generic actors that support a variety of claim-based credential technologies and network-based authentication protocols, thereby giving users a broader choice and facilitating interoperability with service providers. Hence, requirement G2 is satisfied.

The identity broker remains a trusted party in the system. However, as a result of the properties of some claim-based credential technologies, the user's privacy is better protected. This is, for instance, the case in transactions where non-uniquely identifiable information is released. In addition, some authentications are anonymous, making it harder to monitor and link transactions and to compile profiles. Therefore, the architecture positively contributes to requirement U1.

The user agent shows information about the service provider and the requested user attributes during authentication. This allows the user to give his informed consent prior to the disclosure. This satisfies requirement U2.

Requirement U3 is trivially satisfied, since an identity broker in the architecture supports multiple claim-based credential technologies.

A typical Shibboleth identity provider maintains his own data storage, while claim providers in the proposed architecture endorse their provisioned data and thereby convince the identity broker of its correctness. As mentioned in sections 3.3 and 4, service providers can specify a *set of trusted claim providers*. Therefore requirement SP1 is fulfilled.

Furthermore, the identity broker implements a variety of network-based authentication protocols, making it interoperable with many service providers. Therefore, requirement SP2 is fulfilled.

5.2 Discussion

To evaluate differences in trust, we first identify the aspects by which these differences are influenced. Subsequently, we assess the actors to which the identified concerns apply. Finally, we link each of these concerns to the corresponding system actor. The resulting overview is presented in table 1. For the sake of brevity, the term "identity broker" is shortened to *IdB*. The same applies to *IdM* (identity management), *IdP* (identity provider) and *SP* (service provider). To be accurate, we explain the link between the term *issuer* and *identity provider*. This section regards the issuer as an offline identity provider, typically in claim-based systems. However, some of the latter occasionally fetch attributes at authentication-time. Therefore, this division is not always clear-cut. This also explains why such systems might still have some degree of centralised attribute storage. To keep table 1 concise and to avoid unnecessary confusion, we consistently use the term *issuer* for claim-based systems. The T in the table denotes a technology-dependent criterium. For instance, when considering user consent in PKI-based systems, the PIN-based authentication in the German eID enables user consent upon attribute disclosure. The Belgian eID, on the other hand, does not implement this measure. User consent in claim-based systems and in the proposed architecture, is often enforced by a combination of middleware and tamperproof hardware. Selective disclosure in network-based systems (if any), typically involves little user control. Improvements are provided by extensions such as uApprove (Shibboleth) and SimpleSAMLphp. Transactions in network-based systems are often linkable if no anonymous authentication or pseudonym change is supported.

The trust requirements are treated in the last three rows of the table. In network-based systems, we observe strong a trust concentration in a single actor. Claim-based systems demand no trust in two out of three concerns. The proposed architecture has two important merits in this respect. Not only does it reduce the required user trust concerning profiling, transaction linking and impersonation. It also distributes the required trust over multiple actors.

An inherent advantage of the interoperability design criterium, is that the architecture allows identity brokers to use *existing credential infrastructure* to obtain required user attributes. This can prove benefical to the numerous eID architectures that have been deployed over the during the previous years.

5.3 Comparison to Existing Systems

5.4 Extensions

Prototype Extensions. The description of the second prototype setup in section 4.1, mentions that the QR code contains the ID of the session that is to be authenticated, which is a simplified configuration for demo purposes. In real-life setups, this configuration is prone to session hijacking (e.g. a bystander inconspicuously scanning the barcode at a distance). Therefore, the prototype uses a random *authentication id*, of which the mapping to the corresponding session id is kept at the server side.

Section 4.1 also mentions the authentication step where the user is redirected to the Shibboleth Discovery Service, where he can select his preferred identity broker. Considerable anti-phishing protection can be put in place if this preference is preconfigured instead having to select it each time. Little repetitive effort is required for this purpose, considering the generic nature of identity brokers.

In the prototype (section 4.1), the user agent receives the authentication challenge via a QR code, while the response is sent back through the device's Internet connection. Different alternatives are possible, however. For instance, an NFC or Bluetooth technology can be used for both the in- and outbound communication

Table 1. Comparison to existing systems

	NETWORK-BASED IdM	CLAIM-BASED IdM		HYBRID ARCH.	
		PKI	Anon. cred.	PKI	Anon. cred.
User consent	Some systems	T	Yes	T	Yes
Selective disclosure	Some systems	T	Yes	T	Yes
Attribute storage	Centralised	Credential (+ centralised)	Credential	Credential (+ centralised)	Credential
Linkability towards IdP / IdB (best case)	Yes	T	No	No	No
Linkability towards SP (best case)	Often	T	No	No	No
Trust factors: concerns and actors					
SP concern: registration & issuance	IdP	Issuer		Claim provider	
SP concern: authentication & prerequisite fulfillment	IdP	-		IdB	
User concern: no profiling, transaction linking, impersonation	IdP	-		IdB	

with the user agent. Taking advantage of the Internet connection of a different device, is also a possible option.

Enforcing trustworthy execution, is another issue to be taken into account. Browser hardening can be applied to prevent attacks where malware can trick the user into authenticating an illegitimate session or where malware piggybacks on the user's session. Trustworthiness can additionally be enforced on device running the user agent, to safeguard the integrity of the middleware.

Future plans for prototype implementation include the integration and evaluation of new credential technologies as well as authentication protocols other than Shibboleth.

Different Setups. Interesting further research of the proposed approach, may include full integration of a trustworthy identity broker on the smartphone. This will most likely involve the application of tamperproof hardware.

The latter may also be applied at the identity broker's side, to further reduce required trust in this actor. Simultaneously, this would provide more privacy to otherwise less privacy-friendly credential technologies (e.g. X509 certificates).

6 Conclusions

This paper has presented a hybrid architecture that combines network-based and claim-based identity management architectures, leveraging multiple strengths of both and mitigating many of the weaknesses.

The approach offers improved trust, privacy and security properties, compared to several network-based systems, while claim-based identity management systems benefit from a greater extent of interoperability and standardisation, which are more prevalent in the network-based identity management ecosystem.

Additionally, a prototype demonstrates the feasibility of the proposed approach.

Acknowledgements. This work is made possible through funding from the MobCom project, by the Flemish *agency for Innovation by Science and Technology (IWT)*. In this context, we also thankfully mention our joint collaboration with our fellow-researchers from the Steinbuch Centre for Computing, at the Karlsruhe Institute of Technology.

References

1. Mobile security card se 1.0, http://www.gd-sfs.com/the-mobile-security-card/mobile-security-card-se-1-0/
2. Alpár, G., Hoepman, J.-H., Siljee, J.: The identity crisis. security, privacy and usability issues in identity management. CoRR, abs/1101.0427 (2011)
3. Alsaleh, M., Adams, C.: Enhancing Consumer Privacy in the Liberty Alliance Identity Federation and Web Services Frameworks. In: Danezis, G., Golle, P. (eds.) PET 2006. LNCS, vol. 4258, pp. 59–77. Springer, Heidelberg (2006)
4. Bauer, M., Meints, M.M.H.: D3.1: Structured overview on prototypes and concepts of identity management systems. Technical report, FIDIS (2005)
5. Bender, J.: The german eID-Card. presentation (September 2009)
6. Bender, J., Kügler, D., Margraf, M., Naumann, I.: Sicherheitsmechanismen für kontaktlose chips im deutschen elektronischen personalausweis - ein Überblick über sicherheitsmerkmale, risiken, und gegenmassnahmen. Datenschutz und Datensicherheit 32(3), 173–177 (2008)
7. Brands, S.A.: Rethinking Public Key Infrastructures and Digital Certificates: Building in Privacy, 1st edn. MIT Press, Cambridge (2000)
8. Brands, S.A.: The problem(s) with openid. webpage (August. 2007)
9. Camenisch, J., Krontiris, I., Lehmann, A., Neven, G., Paquin, C., Rannenberg, K., Zwingelberg, H.: D2. 1 architecture for attribute-based credential Technologies-Version. Technical report, ABC4Trust Consortium (December 2011), https://abc4trust.eu/index.php/pub/107-d21architecturerev1
10. Camenisch, J., Van Herreweghen, E.: Design and implementation of the *idemix* anonymous credential system. In: ACM Conference on Computer and Communications Security, pp. 21–30 (2002)
11. Chadwick, D.W.: Federated Identity Management. In: Aldini, A., Barthe, G., Gorrieri, R. (eds.) Foundations of Security Analysis and Design V, pp. 96–120. Springer, Heidelberg (2009)

12. De Cock, D., Wolf, C., Preneel, B.: The belgian electronic identity card (overview). In: Sicherheit, pp. 298–301 (2006)

13. Dodson, B., Sengupta, D., Boneh, D., Lam, M.S.: Secure, Consumer-Friendly Web Authentication and Payments with a Phone. In: Gris, M., Yang, G. (eds.) Mobi-CASE 2010. LNICST, vol. 76, pp. 17–38. Springer, Heidelberg (2012)

14. Orawiwattanakul, et al.: User-controlled privacy protection with attribute-filter mechanism for a federated sso environment using shibboleth. In: Proceedings of 3PGCIC 2010, pp. 243–249. IEEE Computer Society Press, Washington, DC (2010)

15. Feld, S., Pohlmann, N.: Security analysis of openid, followed by a reference implementation of an npa-based openid provider. In: Pohlmann, N., Reimer, H., Schneider, W. (eds.) ISSE 2010 Securing Electronic Business Processes, pp. 13–25. Vieweg+Teubner (2011)

16. Leicher, A., Schmidt, A.U., Shah, Y.: Smart OpenID: A Smart Card Based OpenID Protocol. In: Gritzalis, D., Furnell, S., Theoharidou, M. (eds.) SEC 2012. IFIP AICT, vol. 376, pp. 75–86. Springer, Heidelberg (2012)

17. Morgan, R.L., Cantor, S., Carmody, S., Hoehn, W., Klingenstein, K.: Federated security: The shibboleth approach. EDUCAUSE Quarterly 27(4) (2004)

18. Pashalidis, A., Mitchell, C.: A Taxonomy of Single Sign-on Systems. In: Safavi-Naini, R., Seberry, J. (eds.) ACISP 2003. LNCS, vol. 2727, pp. 219–219. Springer, Heidelberg (2003)

19. Recordon, D., Reed, D.: OpenID 2.0: a platform for user-centric identity management. In: DIM 2006: Proceedings of the Second ACM Workshop on Digital Identity Management, pp. 11–16. ACM, New York (2006)

20. International Telecommunication Union. Series y: Global information infrastructure, internet protocol aspects and next-generation networks: Next generation networks - security. Recommendation ITU-T Y.2720, International Telecommunication Union (2010)

21. Verslype, K.: Improving Privacy in Applications by Managing the Disclosed Personal Properties. PhD thesis, Katholieke Universiteit Leuven (March 2011)

22. Vossaert, J., Lapon, J., De Decker, B., Naessens, V.: User-Centric Identity Management Using Trusted Modules. In: Camenisch, J., Lambrinoudakis, C. (eds.) EuroPKI 2010. LNCS, vol. 6711, pp. 155–170. Springer, Heidelberg (2011)

23. Wikipedia. Id-wsf - wikipedia. webpage (May 2012)

24. Wikipedia. Shibboleth - wikipedia. webpage (May 2012)

Program Structure-Based Feature Selection for Android Malware Analysis

Andrew Walenstein[1], Luke Deshotels[2], and Arun Lakhotia[2]

[1] Center for Advanced Computer Studies, University of Louisiana at Lafayette,
Lafayette, LA 70504, U.S.A
arun@louisiana.edu, alecdeshotels@gmail.com
[2] School of Computing and Informatics, University of Louisiana at Lafayette,
Lafayette, LA 70504, U.S.A
walenste@ieee.org

1 Introduction

Zhou and Jiang [1] extensively surveyed and analyzed Android malware and found that 86% of the malware collected incorporated repackaged benign applications, and that many of them utilized common advertisement libraries. Such benign code reuse in malware can be expected to cause automated classification and clustering approaches to fail if they base their decisions on features relating to the reused code. To improve detection, classification, and clustering, *feature selection* from mobile malware must not be naïve, but must instead utilize knowledge of malicious program semantics and structure. We propose an approach for selecting features of mobile malware by using knowledge of malicious program structure to heuristically identify malicious portions of applications.

2 Program Structure-Based Feature Selection Approach

We propose to restrict feature selection to only those components within an Android app that are likely to be malicious as indicated by program structure. Potential components of interest are found by selecting all classes with methods that are *receivers* of *intents*: these are methods that receive control from the Android platform in response to broadcast events. That is, they are "entry points" to the receiving components. A receiving component is labeled as suspicious if it is isolated from the rest of the program. Isolation of the receiving components is ranked using the network centrality [2] measure on its program dependence graph [3]. Known benign advertisement libraries that also match this pattern of isolation are removed from consideration. Suspicious classes are labeled as a malicious component and features are selected only from these components.

3 Study of Automated Classification of Android Malware

An 11-file sub-sample of Android malware from the Android Malware Genome Project [1] was selected to illustrate the problem of poor clustering due to naïve

A.U. Schmidt et al. (Eds.): MOBISEC 2012, LNICST 107, pp. 51–52, 2012.

feature selection. Samples from four "families" of malware were selected such that some files shared repackaged apps (ADRD and Pjapps-b) or shared benign libraries (DroidKungFu and DroidDreamLight).

Each file was disassembled, the program dependence graph extracted, and the suspicious component was extracted using our proposed heuristic strategy. From each suspicious component, all *signatures* (with full type information) of all method calls were extracted, and the pairwise Jaccard similarity scores between each set of calls was computed. Automated hierarchical agglomerative clustering was then performed on the similarity matrix using CLUTO [4]. Two treatments were utilized: the naïve one where features consisted of all method calls from the entire app, and the proposed heuristic selection method where the features consisted of method calls originating only in the suspicious component. Results for both treatments are shown below, with the generated hierarchy drawn on the left hand side and the associated similarity matrix visualized to its right. The 11 by 11 matrices visualize the pairwise Jaccard similarity scores; darker squares show higher similarity, and rows and columns are laid out in the same order. Each similarity matrix is divided into four classes automatically.

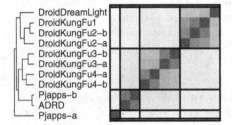   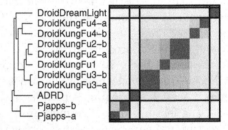

Naive selection treatment   Heuristic selection treatment

The results illustrate how the heuristic feature selection might help improve clustering or classification performance. In the naïve case Pjapps-b and ADRD are inappropriately clustered together, likely because they share a common repackaged app, and the DroidKungFu1 sub-tree clusters closer to DroidDreamLight than the DroidKungFu2 sub-tree. The heuristic selection changes the similarity scores so that within-class similarity are generally higher, between-class similarities are generally lower, and the resulting clusters match the ground truth precisely.

References

1. Zhou, Y., Jiang, X.: Dissecting Android malware: Characterization and evolution. In: Proceedings of the 33rd IEEE Symposium on Security and Privacy, Oakland, CA, U.S.A (May 2012)
2. Brandes, U.: A faster algorithm for betweenness centrality. J. of Mathematical Sociology 25(2), 163–177 (2001)
3. Ferrante, J., Ottenstein, K.J., Warren, J.D.: The program dependence graph and its use in optimization. ACM Trans. Program. Lang. Syst. 9(3), 319–349 (1987)
4. Karypis, G.: CLUTO – A clustering toolkit. Technical Report TR 02–017, Department of Computer Science, U. of Minnesota (November 2003)

Presenting the Brazilian Project TSAM – Security Technologies for Mobile Environments

Alexandre M. Braga, Erick N. Nascimento, and Lucas R. Palma

Fundação CPqD – Centro de Pesquisa e Desenvolvimento em Telecomunicações,
Rodovia Campinas - Mogi-Mirim (SP-340) , km 118,5
CEP 13086-902 - Campinas, SP - Brazil
{ambraga,erick,lpalma}@cpqd.com.br

Abstract. In 2010, the number of mobile phones exceeded the size of Brazilian population, when Brazil has achieved the important mark of 200 million mobile accesses, about 40 million of them for data accesses. During the last quarter of 2011, project TSAM has started with a planned duration of 36 months and the main goal of providing security technologies for mobile environments, concerning secure communication, secure assessments and malware analysis.

Keywords: Mobile security, secure mobile communication, Android security.

1   Introduction

Mobile devices, especially smartphones and tablets, are the protagonists of a silent revolution, characterized by the use of devices with high processing power and connectivity in public and private networks. The aggregation of such characteristics to the wide pervasiveness of these devices brings a whole new set of threats. According to the Brazilian Telecommunications Agency, in 2010 the number of mobile accesses has exceeded the number of people in Brazil [1], about 40 million being data [1].

This extended abstract presents Project TSAM – Tecnologias de Segurança para Ambientes Móveis – which stands for Security Technologies for Mobile Environments. The main motivation for the project is to offer technological solutions for the growing demand for security in mobile environments. This demand was caused not only by the significant increase in the use of smart mobile devices (smartphones and tablets), but also by the cyber criminals growing interest in mobile environments. It's worth noting the existence of malicious software specific to the Brazilian context, according to the Computer Security Incident Response Team (CSIRT) for the Brazilian Internet [2].

The results obtained so far are influencing the structure of a laboratory for mobile security, which will be able to carry out assessments on mobile environments, including platforms, applications and communications. Also, it was observed two interesting facts concerning mobile environments in Brazil: (i) the Android's increasing relevance, attracting the interest of government agencies, financial institutions, telecom operators, and enterprises; (ii) an increase in the exploitation of vulnerabilities of mobile devices in general and of Android in particular.

A.U. Schmidt et al. (Eds.): MOBISEC 2012, LNICST 107, pp. 53–54, 2012.
© Institute for Computer Sciences, Social Informatics and Telecommunications Engineering 2012

2   Project Overview and Preliminary Results

The TSAM project was designed around three main objectives. The first one is to build secure data communication prototypes as well as secure voice over data packets (or over IP), both of them through smartphones on public networks (s.t. 3G, 4G, wifi). The second one is to develop tools for integrity checking on smartphones, as well as techniques for active investigation of security incidents and penetration tests on mobile platforms. Finally, the third objective is to build an environment for experimentation, observation and analysis of mobile malware.

During the project's specification, it has been identified that the opportunities for research and innovative development on mobile security come from efficient implementation of cryptography for VoIP communication on smartphones and tablets [4, 5], as well as mobile security assessment and mobile malware analysis [3]. Android was chosen as the preferred platform for development of prototypes. The efforts are now directed to Android, on three short-term goals: (i) experiments on the portability of cryptographic libraries, (ii) definition of a software architecture for secure instant messages, and (iii) composition of security tools on a test suite.

3   Concluding Remarks

The beginning of the project occurs at a moment when mobile devices increases their market share in relation to other personal computing devices, resulting in increased interest in exploiting technical vulnerabilities of these devices. This research group is looking for collaboration opportunities in the area of mobile security with well-established groups abroad.

Acknowledgments. The authors acknowledge the financial support given to this work, under the project "Security Technologies for Mobile Environments – TSAM", granted by the Fund for Technological Development of Telecommunications – FUNTTEL – of the Brazilian Ministry of Communications, through Agreement Nr. 01.11. 0028.00 with the Financier of Studies and Projects - FINEP / MCTI.

References

1. ANATEL – Agência Nacional de Telecomunicações, http://www.anatel.gov.br
2. CERT.br – Centro de Estudos, Resposta e Tratamento de Incidentes de Segurança no Brasil, http://www.cert.br
3. Enck, W., Octeau, D., McDaniel, P., Chaudhuri, S.: A study of android application security. In: Proceedings of the 20th USENIX Conference on Security, SEC 2011 (2011)
4. NSA. Enterprise Mobility Architecture for Secure Voice over Internet Protocol. Mobility Capability Package – Secure VoIP, Version 1.2
5. Grosschadl, J., Page, D.: Efficient Java Implementation of Elliptic Curve Cryptography for J2ME-Enabled Mobile Devices. Cryptology ePrint Archive, Report Nr. 2011/712 (2011)

Scalable Trust Assessment and Remediation
of Wireless Devices

Andreas Leicher[1], Andreas U. Schmidt[1], and Yogendra Shah[2]

[1] Novalyst IT AG, Robert-Bosch-Straße 38, 61184 Karben, Germany
{andreas.schmidt,andreas.leicher}@novalyst.de
[2] InterDigital Communications, LLC, 781 Third Ave, King of Prussia, PA 19406

In large scale deployments of partly autonomously communicating and connecting network elements, such as the Internet of Things and machine-to-machine devices, trust issues have new qualities. Concurrently, end-user devices are technically open platforms, and also pose security threats on a large scale to users and networks. Thus, fault detection and remediation methods become costly. It is a key challenge to balance the requirements of scalability and cost-effectiveness with desired fine-grained checks and remote remediation. Current technologies, such as Trusted Computing Group's Trusted Network Connect and Open Mobile Alliance's Device Management Standards, may not be an ideal fit to the requirements. Extensions like property-based attestation (PBA) are promising, but may require special infrastructure and/or further standardization. We consider an architecture for Platform Validation and Management (PVM) in which designated network entities protect the access network by remotely validating devices before they are allowed to authenticate and gain access. We propose methods to diagnose devices with a granularity which allows also attachment even with partial functionality and methods to remediate faulty devices remotely, i.e., bring them back into a known good state. This approach requires some separation of tasks between network PVM entities and trusted functionalities on devices [1, 2]. Our generic and efficient approach to PVM, rests on three key ingredients:

First, A trusted platform architecture allowing separation of the system in a Secure Execution Environment (SEE) and a Normal Execution Environment (NEE). The system is capable of performing a secure start-up (bootstrap) process anchored in a Root of Trust (RoT) and building a chain of trust from the RoT to SEE to NEE, verifying start-up, particularly started components against Trusted Reference Values (TRVs). This is an abstraction of the Trusted Computing Group's MPWG (Mobile Phone WG) Platform Architecture, which may be mapped to many different, concrete architectures.

Second, In a PVM architecture, only 'good/trustworthy' devices may gain (partial or full) access to the network. The platform undergoes a remote validation procedure before or while authenticating. In case the platform or parts of it fail validation, the platform shall be granted partial access or quarantined and remediated. For this, the platform runs, after secure start-up, an interactive interrogation procedure with the PVM Server, to determine which components have failed integrity check during

A.U. Schmidt et al. (Eds.): MOBISEC 2012, LNICST 107, pp. 55–56, 2012.

start-up and require remediation, e.g. by replacing them. The interrogation protocol consists of a sequence of short messages to 'zoom in with the desired granularity', on failed components. The PVM server prepares a remediation/update code package and pushes it to the device, which then restarts.

Third, the key to making PVM efficient is a method to find specific faults in the set of measured components, called Tree-Formed Validation, which enables fast search for failed components (a logarithmic speed-up compared to a linear search). Integrity measurements taken on components are stored in a Merkle hash tree instead of a linear log file. The root cryptographically protects it's leafs representing component measurements. Interactive interrogation with the PVM server descends the levels of the tree [3].

We have built a demonstration consisting of a virtual user device – e.g. an Android smart phone – residing in a host system which represents the secure environment. The SEE contains an emulated TPM, extended by custom functionality to build and manage tree-formed integrity verification data (employing an Integrity Verification Capability, IVC) and to interact with the PVM server (via a Remediation Capability, RC). At start-up, the SEE verifies and starts the Trusted Computing Base (TCB) of the Android device, including a Measurement Agent which then measures and starts components, driven by a policy provided from the SEE. The measurement agent delivers integrity measurement values to the IVC in the SEE, which performs storage in the measurement tree using the TFV-extended TPM functionality. If, after start-up and measurement of all components, the root of any tree measurement log fails to verify against the corresponding TRV (a check performed by the IVC), the IVC triggers remediation with the PVM server via the RC.

Remote validation and remediation with the PVM server is performed by descending a measurement tree interactively: In every validation message from RC to PVM server, two child values of the current tree node under consideration are transferred until a failing leaf is reached. By depth-first search, every failing component is identified and ultimately replaced.

References

1. Schmidt, A.U., Cha, I., Shah, Y., Leicher, A., Meyerstein, M.: Trust in M2M Communications. IEEE Vehicular Technology Magazine 4(3), 69–75 (2009)
2. Schmidt, A.U., Cha, I., Shah, Y., Leicher, A.: Trusted Platform Validation and Management. International Journal of Dependable and Trustworthy Information Systems (IJDTIS) 1(2), 1–31 (2010)
3. Schmidt, A.U., Leicher, A., Shah, Y., Cha, I.: Tree-formed Verification Data for Trusted Platforms, http://arxiv.org/abs/1007.0642v3

Verifying the Location of a Mobile Device User

Jack Brassil and Pratyusa K. Manadhata

HP Laboratories

Abstract. Certain location-based services seek to spontaneously authenticate user location without the need to have a pre-existing relationship with each user, or with each location provider. We introduce an intelligent infrastructure-based solution that provides spontaneous, rapid, and robust mobile device location authentication by supplementing existing 802.11x APs with femtocells. We show that by transferring data to a mobile device associated with a femtocell while remotely monitoring its traffic activity, a sender can verify the cooperating receiver's location. We explain how to design data transmissions with distinct traffic signatures that can be rapidly and reliably detected even in the presence of heavy cross-traffic introduced by other femtocell users. Neither mobile operators nor location providers need be aware that an authentication is taking place.

Keywords: Distance bounding, GPS, indoor positioning, location privacy.

1 Introduction

The combination of handset-based and mobile operator network-based location services have stimulated the emergence of a growing number of compelling location services. Yet neither type of location service is ideally suited to address the needs of many internet-based Location-based Application Providers (LAPs), ranging from discount distributors such as *LivingSocial* and *GroupOn* to geosocial services including *foursquare*. Many LAPs not only seek to locate clients, but also authenticate those client locations. In many cases, those clients are new users of the LAP's service with whom they have no pre-existing relationship, such as a consumer entering a shopping mall.

Few options are available to LAPs to spontaneously authenticate a new client; mobile operators provide ubiquitously available network-based location services, though these services are targeted at their subscribers, and operators are unable, unauthorized or simply reluctant to provide subscriber location information to third parties who are not partners (e.g., E-911).

As a result inexpensive and widely deployed GPS receivers have made handset-based location service the preferred choice of LAPs. Existing services generally rely on a user's assertion of location (e.g., via an application uploading GPS coordinates). But the economic incentives for users to provide false location information are growing, as evidenced by the growing number of location spoofing

A.U. Schmidt et al. (Eds.): MOBISEC 2012, LNICST 107, pp. 57–68, 2012.

apps available on the Android market. As a result, a discounter such as *Cheap Sally* is unable to report to its advertisers that all coupons that were distributed went to mobile consumers whose locations were authenticated.

Other potential applications of mobile user location authentication are both diverse and expanding. Conventional Location-Based Access Control (LBAC) systems limit access to sensitive information systems from only known, authorized sites (e.g., fixed banking institution locations). But the rise of mobile computing and telecommuting has increased demand for limited access permissions to be granted to off-site workers and customers.

To address the desire to create a public location authentication infrastructure we have proposed to place femtocells at existing public WiFi sites [1]. The short wireless range of these basestations permits us to locate associated User Equipment (UE) to within tens of meters, and indoor operation is supported. In this paper we show how *data* traffic can be used to impress a traffic signature at a femtocell to authenticate user location. Our key contributions include 1) a lightweight non-cryptographic method of verifying an untrusted party's location; 2) an authentication architecture requiring no modifications to existing mobile handsets, operator infrastructure, or public APs, and not requiring trusted infrastructure; and 3) the ability to authenticate locations while keeping the located party's and the verifier's identities unknown to the location service provider.

The remainder of the paper is organized as follows. Section 2 describes our design goals. The next section provides a brief refresher on femtocell technology, then outlines our proposed authentication system architecture and operation. We also examine the problem of designing and detecting traffic signatures in the presence of interfering cross-traffic including voice calls, text messages and data transfers introduced by other femtocell users. We present a security analysis in Section 4, where we describe plausible attacks and attempts to defeat our system, with and without collusion. In the final sections we summarize our contributions, and identify several envisioned enhancements of our authentication approach.

2   Design Goals

Consider a LAP that seeks to authenticate a previously unknown client's current location. Suppose that the client carries a 'smart' mobile device, but the LAP has no knowledge of the client's mobile operator or device capabilities. The LAP requires a *spontaneous, one-time* authentication. A new client might be moving, and a verification transaction must be fast and involve minimal client engagement. Few restrictions should be placed on potential clients, so authentication must be 1) *device-independent* – including basic phones, smartphones, and tablets, and 2) *carrier-independent* – including devices spanning different data transmission technologies including 3G and LTE.

The location service itself should offer fine-grain location information – perhaps equivalent to GPS, while supporting both indoor and outdoor operation. The service must be trusted by the LAP. The system should be sufficiently *hard* for the client *to defeat* but need not be *unbreakable*, as determined by a LAP's *investments* in the transaction, e.g., a discount retail coupon's value and an unauthorized system access's cost.

Security and privacy requirements are also paramount. Clients must *opt-in* to each location verification. In some cases the client might seek to mutually-authenticate the LAP. Finally, the transaction itself should take place with a high-degree of client location *privacy*. Where possible, the location service provider should be unaware that a location verification even took place, and no records need be kept. Indeed, authorized authentications should occur while the located party and the verifier remain entirely anonymous to the LAP.

Of course, these design goals are not rigid requirements, and serve only as a starting point to characterize the needs of a wide variety of LAPs. Though our set of system goals seems potentially unachievable, in the next section we will show how they can be realized. Intriguingly, despite the use of femtocells our solution does not entail mobile operators providing the location service at all.

3   A Public Location Authentication System

To perform a location authentication we supplement existing public Wifi hotspots with off-the-shelf femtocells. We rely on various femtocell properties (e.g., limited transmission range, exposed uplink, private ownership, integrated GPS) to authenticate the location of a femtocell-associated mobile device, without requiring mobile operator involvement or any modifications to operator infrastructure or services.

Femtocells [2] are low-power, limited range (e.g., tens of meters) wireless access points that operate in licensed spectrum to connect subscriber's mobile devices to their mobile operator's network. Femtocells typically use wired public internet access as backhaul. They satisfy the various regulatory, compliance and spectrum use requirements of macrocells, including supporting location service. Femtocells were introduced to improve cellular coverage inside buildings and areas with relatively poor cell tower coverage. Residential femtocells typically support only 2-8 active mobile device associations (i.e., users), while emerging enterprise femtocells can support 8-32 active users.

Voice calls can originate on residential femtocells, and subsequently be handed over to cell towers as callers move, however active calls originating elsewhere may not be handed to a femtocell. Inter-femtocell handoffs are supported in enterprise equipment where dense access point coverage is desired. Femtocell owners may specify access control lists (e.g., family members only, any subscriber). GPS signal availability is typically required, and can be achieved in indoor devices through cabled remote antennas. In most ways a femtocell is best viewed as remotely managed and largely closed infrastructure that happens to reside on customer premises.

Voice and data traffic to and from the femtocell are directed to a Security Gateway (SG) at the edge of the operator's core network. Some control traffic may also be directed to other service points, such as a GPS Gateway. Voice, data

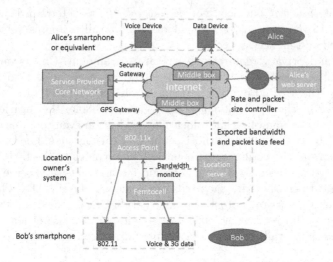

Fig. 1. Architecture of a single-carrier system capable of authenticating smartphone location. A multi-carrier system would employ one femtocell for each mobile operator.

and control traffic between the mobile operator's core network and femtocell is tunneled and encrypted with the Encapsulated Security Payload (ESP) protocol [3], and transported over UDP. Hence, confidentiality is assured against exactly the passive monitoring that we will describe in the next section.

3.1   System Architecture and Operation

We now introduce the participants in a location authentication. *Bob* is a smart mobile device user whose location is to be authenticated. He is willing to co-operate with the authentication to realize some benefit but *Alice* can not trust his assertion of his location. Alice seeks to verify Bob's present location (with his explicit approval). Alice and Bob do not need to have any pre-existing relationship; Alice could be a LAP unknown to Bob. Alice must have the equivalent capability of a smart phone, or more precisely a (mobile or landline) voice-only phone plus minimal compute and display capability; a web browser suffices. The *Location Service Provider* (LSP) seeks to provide a public-access location authentication service. The location itself – say a coffee shop – might already offer a public WiFi service. The site location is assumed to be fixed over time. The LSP – the coffee shop owner – has no prior relationship with either Alice or Bob, each of who can remain permanently anonymous to the LSP.

Figure 1 depicts the basic authentication system architecture; the specific implementation details of the prototype system we constructed are found in [4]. To an existing 802.11x access point with an internet connection, an LSP minimally adds 1) a femtocell, and 2) a computer operating as a *location server*. The location server hosts a web server, and offers a public page with detailed site location information (e.g., GPS, postal address, contact information, etc.) The location server also continuously monitors 1) the average bandwidth, and

2) the packet lengths on the (encrypted) downlink between the AP and femtocell; an average bandwidth for each 1 second interval is measured, and these values form a data stream that is publicly exported. Note that the computational burden of the location server is sufficiently small that in practice it can be run directly on either the AP or the femtocell. Internet middleboxes might exist between Alice and Bob, limiting her ability to use network geo-location techniques to locate him.

The figure also depicts Bob's mobile Service Provider's core network. Alice need not share a common operator network with Bob, nor even know Bob's operator. Regardless of source, any voice or data communication from Alice to Bob will ultimately traverse Bob's operator's network on route to Bob. Bob must have a data-capable device such as a smartphone or mobile computer, and Alice must be capable of controlling her data transfer's network traffic characteristics (e.g., transmission rate, packet lengths). The data can be pushed or pulled, and the underlying transfer protocol is unrestricted. One simple approach that is consistent with our design objectives – namely mobile device independence and mobile user opt-in – is for Alice to provide Bob the URL of a data file on a web server she controls, and allow Bob to initiate the data transfer. Note that *http* transfers potentially avoid the need for Bob to have a special-purpose application to receive the transfer.

Assume that Bob is in range of the LSP's femtocell. Note, of course, that other subscribers of Bob's mobile operator might be present at the location, be associated with the femtocell, and also might be receiving voice and data traffic through the femtocell. But many of those present will likely select the available higher-bandwidth Wifi data service, and opt less for data service through the femtocell channel. Consider the following basic authentication process:

1. Bob successfully binds to the femtocell.
2. Bob messages Alice, and provides her with the LSP's location URL.
3. The location server continuously monitors the (encrypted) AP-femto downstream link and exports two (logical) streams: 1) the average bandwidth over each one second interval, and 2) the number of packets received in the previous second of each observed packet length.
4. Alice transfers data to Bob and controls either the transfer rate or packet lengths (or both) to impress a unique traffic signature on the AP-femto link.
5. Alice monitors the exported bandwidth feed for characteristics of her data transfer.

Of course, these operations can be automated and need not be performed manually. When Alice communicates with Bob, she expects the bandwidth measured on the femtocell ingress to increase and expects the bandwidth to fall when she terminates communication.

– If the behavior of the bandwidth feed convinces Alice that she is observing her own traffic traverse the AP-femtocell link, Alice confirms Bob's phone's association with the femtocell, and concludes that Bob is present at the specified location.

– If the observed bandwidth feed does not reflect Alice's communications, she can not conclude that Bob is on-site. Alice can elect to retry her authentication transfer at a later time to confirm Bob's presence.

Of course, other coffee shop occupants might also be transferring data, or receiving voice calls using the femtocell. In the following sections we will describe how Alice can design a data transfer such that she can reliably detect the presence or absence of her call, even when competing with significant cross-traffic from other users of the AP-femto link.

3.2   Authenticating with Data Transfers

We next consider the problems of 1) the design of the network traffic Alice chooses to use to serve as her *fingerprint* that she is indeed using the AP-femto link, and 2) extracting that signal from other cross-traffic generated by femtocell users on site (e.g., voice calls, text messages, data transfers), and consequently verifying Bob's presence at that site.

To begin, consider the cross-traffic characteristics. An active voice call has a well-defined traffic characteristic, and it appears as a relatively long duration, continuous data stream of small packets at a rate of approximately 50 kbs, depending on the voice codecs used. Data traffic (e.g., file transfers, web pages, MMS) are typically high bandwidth (e.g., $100-2000$ kbs) bursts of several to tens of seconds duration. Text traffic (i.e., SMS) are typically low bandwidth (e.g., $1-5$ kbs) bursts of similar duration. Even dozens of simultaneously arriving text messages represent insignificant 'noise' in Alice's signal detection. But even a single contemporaneous cross-traffic data transfer can potentially interfere with an authentication transfer.

Alice seeks to create an easily discernible traffic signature that looks entirely unlike this cross-traffic. She performs two actions to modify the characteristics of her transfer. First, she controls the transmission rate such that her traffic stream does not have an bandwidth rate *envelope* similar to cross-traffic. For example, choosing a constant-rate transmission of higher bandwidth than a voice call is unlikely to be mistaken as either a voice call (low rate) or a data transfer (bursty). Such a rate-limited transfer is trivial for Alice to implement. Second, Alice should control the size of her individual packet transmissions. Modifying packet lengths arbitrarily is also easy to control. Her objective is to set each packet size to a randomly-selected, infrequently observed value; this size could be fixed, or could vary over the transfer lifetime. To determine such a value(s), we observe that the typical length distribution for packets arriving to femtocell ingress is bi-modal. Voice traffic comprises almost entirely small packets (e.g., 40-200 bytes), and data transfers are a mix of small (e.g., TCP acknowledgments for outbound data) and large (e.g., 1300 bytes) packets transporting data. Hence Alices chooses a value (or values) in the range of 400-1000 bytes, avoiding a few commonly occurring sizes (e.g., 512 bytes).

Suppose a file transfer normally includes N packets of size greater than 1200 bytes with a path MTU of 1500 bytes. If instead Alice chooses to reduce her

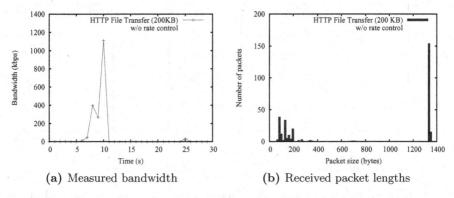

(a) Measured bandwidth   (b) Received packet lengths

Fig. 2. Received bandwidth and packet lengths with no server rate control

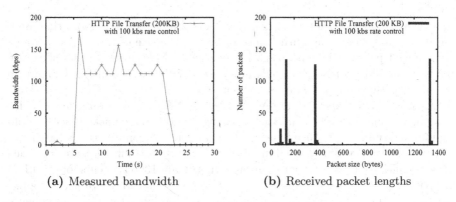

(a) Measured bandwidth   (b) Received packet lengths

Fig. 3. Received bandwidth and packet lengths with 100 kbs server rate control and 1500 byte MTU

packet sizes to a maximum of 550 bytes (e.g., by temporarily setting her server's NIC's MTU to 550), we expect a data transfer to contain approximately $2N$ packets of length approximately 550 bytes. Recall that transfers to the femtocell are encapsulated by the mobile operator, representing a packet length increase of roughly 10% at the ingress link.

Consider the following example. Figure 2a depicts the measured average bandwidths of a high rate web transfer that might represent cross-traffic while Alice is transmitting her authentication signal. Figure 2b shows the numbers of packets at each length for that interfering transfer. As expected, we see a bi-modal distribution of entirely either small or large packets. Figure 3a depicts a rate-controlled transfer from Alice where she does not control packet length. Packets lengths associated with this transfer appear in Figure 3b; here we see approximately equal numbers of packets of two, tightly clustered lengths: large (i.e., 1390 B) and medium-sized (i.e., 390 B). Figure 4a illustrates the same data transmission with Alice electing to both rate-control and set packet size to 512 B for the duration of the transfer. As expected, Figure 4b shows (blue) that we

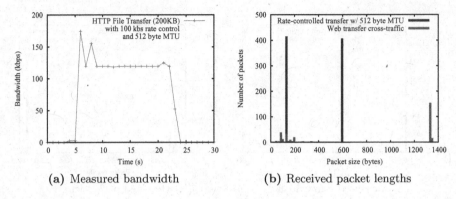

(a) Measured bandwidth   **(b)** Received packet lengths

Fig. 4. Received bandwidth and packet lengths with 100 kbs server rate control and 512 byte MTU

no longer see large packets during the transfer, but instead see more than double their number arriving with length of 590 B, the size of the largest possible transmitted packet with encapsulation overhead. The packet counts shown in red correspond to what Alice would also observe if the web transfer of Figure 2a occurred in the same interval as her authentication transfer. Clearly, a detector looking for the expected largest packet size of Alice's transmissions – in this case the unusual size 590 B suddenly arriving at a rate of 20 packets/sec – would rapidly determine that Alice is using the channel, and confirm Bob's location.

Our observations of femtocell ingress voice and data traffic indicate that each packet length on 16 B boundaries in the range of 600-1300 B occurs for ($\leq 0.1\%$) of arriving packets; most lengths are not observed at all. If desirable, of course, Alice could further improve the reliability of detection by sending a sequence of very short transfers each of which has a distinct, unusual packet length from that range. Such an approach would also strengthen the system from attacks, a topic we discuss in the next section.

4   Security Analysis

We next conduct a security analysis of our system and identify plausible attacks; additional discussion of attacks can be found in [5]. Informally, our system's *attack surface* consists of three actors – Alice, Bob, and the LSP (i.e., store owner) – and six devices – Alice's smartphone, her web server, the LSP's 802.11x access point, the femtocell, the location server, and Bob's smartphone. Hence our system can be attacked if the actors behave maliciously and/or if the devices are compromised. Also, an attacker can disrupt the system's operation via denial-of-service attacks.

Location authentication systems proposed in the literature almost invariably rely on trusted infrastructure, e.g., public key infrastructure (PKI) and trusted platform modules (TPM) (Section 5). Such systems use cryptographic protocols to achieve high confidence in authentication. In contrast, our system places no trust in infrastructure beyond their normal operation and avoids complex trusted infrastructure management, but provides authentication strength consistent with the commercial needs of existing LAPs. Most systems – including ours – however, remain vulnerable to certain attacks, e.g., collusive 'wormhole' attacks, where a remote party colludes with an on-site associate to fake one's presence.

4.1   Deceiving the System

Bob may *fool* our system, i.e., he may prove to Alice that he is near a Location Server (LS) even though he is not; we outline three plausible approaches to deceive our system.

First, Bob may be able to *modify* the length or bandwidth data feed observed by Alice and may impress a fingerprint on the feed so as to indicate his presence near the LS. For example, Bob may compromise the LS and modify the exported data feed, or may modify the bandwidth feed during its transmission from the LS to Alice. Bob, however, has to guess Alice's traffic signature in real time to carry out the attacks. In another difficult real-time attack, Bob may replace both the traffic signal exported by the web server to Alice and the bandwidth feed exported by the LS each with a signal of his choosing. Alice would then observe that the exported data stream has the expected characteristics of her data transfer, and hence believe that Bob is near the LS.

Second, either Bob or the LSP, acting independently or in collusion, may send a phony bandwidth feed to Alice (e.g., by using a fake location URL). We, however, assume that the LSP is unlikely to perform these malicious activities due to economic disincentives; all future economic benefit to the LSP is placed at risk if his malicious activities are detected.

Third, Bob may forward Alice's data file's URL to an on-site colluder (or a colluding LSP) and the colluder may download the file using the LSP's femtocell. The bandwidth feed Alice monitors will now have a fingerprint similar to what she expects, albeit not identical and slightly delayed. The delay, however, may not be decisive for Alice to detect foul play as there will be a legitimate time lag between when Bob receives Alice's URL and when Bob starts downloading the file. Alice may make the delay more easily detectable by *pushing* the data file to Bob instead of him pulling the data file from the URL.

4.2   Disrupting System Operation

Our system is susceptible to *denial-of-service* attacks, i.e., Bob may not be able to prove his location to Alice even if he wanted to. We outline four plausible approaches to disrupt our system's operation.

First, an attacker may modify the bandwidth feed observed by Alice to a feed that is different from Alice's expected bandwidth feed; hence Alice would believe that Bob is not near the LS. For example, as discussed in the previous section, the attacker may compromise the LS, Alice's device, and Alice's web server, or tamper with data transmission to achieve his goal.

Second, an attacker may perform a network DDoS attack on either Alice's network and/or the LS's network, and hence may prevent Alice from accessing the exported data feed and also may prevent Bob from downloading Alice's data file. Both Bob and Alice, however, can easily detect these attacks.

Third, an attacker may simultaneously use many phones at the location to exceed the femtocell's association capacity. Then Bob will be blocked from using the femtocell to receive calls and Alice won't be able to reach Bob.

Fourth, an attacker may compromise our system's components and prevent the components from performing their role. For example, the attacker may prevent the location server from measuring the bandwidth and/or exporting the bandwidth and may prevent Alice's web server from sending the file to Bob.

In the first attack, Alice concludes that Bob is not near the LS even though Bob is. Alice cannot conclude anything about Bob's location in the other attacks; Bob may or may not be near the LS. Hence the first attack is more severe than the rest, but is more difficult to mount.

Lastly, we briefly mention key privacy concerns. An attacker may be able to learn Bob's location by attacking our system. For example, if the attacker compromises Alice's device and gets access to her phone records and web access logs, then the attacker can learn Bob's location. Also, we assume that the LSP's exported data feed is available to any remote party; hence the feed's (in)activity might provide some general indication about the presence/absence of people on site, a potential security risk.

5   Related Work

Despite considerable research time and effort [6,7], authenticating mobile client location remains difficult. Classical authentication system proposals often relied on distance bounding [8], whereas recent proposals use PKIs and TPMs. Our approach is similar to related work in two aspects. First, in principle, we assume that we trust an entity's location and then prove that a mobile device is near the entity; the entity could be a femtocell or an 802.11x AP [9,10]. Second, in implementation, we extend existing infrastructure by adding femtocells and location servers. In comparison, prior work requires certification authorities [11], APs capable of issuing cryptographic location proofs [9,10], and trusted platform modules (TPM) [12,13,14]. Our approach, however, differs in one key aspect: we don't use any cryptographic primitives and rely on lightweight traffic signals for authentication.

Dua et al. [12], Saroiu & Wolman [13], and Gilbert et al. [14] use TPMs to protect the integrity of sensor data. TPMs, however, are not generally found in existing mobile devices. Moreover, the location sensing device inputs remain vulnerable to manipulation, e.g., using GPS signal simulators. Several proposals extend an AP's basic functionality to support location authentication; Luo & Hengartner [9] and Saroiu & Wolman [10] propose solutions that involve APs capable of issuing location proofs. Faria and Cheriton [15] introduce an authentication architecture using a group of APs controlled by a centralized wireless appliance.

Some research on location authentication cleverly exploits channel observations in broadcast wireless networks (e.g., broadcast packets [16], [17], modulated power [18]) to form shared secrets to establish user proximity to an AP. Also, reputation systems [19] and Near-Field Communications [20] have been explored for location based access control.

WiFi Positioning Systems (WPS) and hybrid WPS/GPS systems (e.g., Skyhook Wireless [21]), though popular for indoor/outdoor location determination, are vulnerable to location-spoofing and denial-of-service attacks [22]. More recently, *location-as-a-service* startups (e.g., LOC-AID [23]) have begun to serve as intermediaries between mobile operators and third parties seeking client location. While promising, bootstrapping these services is challenging; each client and third party must proactively establish a relationship with each aggregator.

6   Conclusion

We have proposed and demonstrated a novel approach to infrastructure-based location authentication that operates in a spontaneous, transaction-oriented fashion in public settings. Our approach strives to be well aligned with the evolving needs of internet location-based application providers, and particularly their desire to authenticate new users rapidly and robustly.

Many possible embellishments of our basic system proposal are straightforward, e.g., a multi-femtocell configuration to support more users in a small physical space. Multi-carrier operation can be achieved by simply arraying femtocells from each service provider. Digital signatures should be employed in transfers to authenticate Bob's presence, not just the presence of his smartphone. Femtocells are, of course, not widely deployed today, as would be required to scale our system. But, apart from enabling new services, the basic advantages of wider deployment of femtocell technology – both to operators and consumers – remain plentiful. Our system requires no changes to operator infrastructure or mobile user equipment. Hence, the technology required to deploy a large-scale location authentication system exists, is inexpensive, operates off-the-shelf, and can be deployed incrementally. While future large-scale deployment of femtocells is uncertain, we do envision the integration of femtocell and 802.11x radios in a single multi-access unit as being a potential catalyst for wider-scale deployment. Though our authentication scheme is not foolproof, it appears to be sufficiently difficult-to-defeat to support the modest authentication requirements of emerging internet LAPs.

Our system exploits mobile-operator technology without actually involving the operator directly in a transaction. Yet we believe that more robust authentications can be achieved with the mobile operator's active involvement. In particular, operators control the infrastructure, have preferential network vantage points, and can create easily discernible authentication fingerprints.

Acknowledgment. The authors would like to acknowledge contributions from R. Netravali, S. Haber, and P. Rao.

References

1. Netravali, R., Brassil, J.: Femtocell-assisted Location Authentication (poster/extended abstract). In: IEEE LANMAN 2011 (October 2011)
2. Chandrasekhar, V., Andrews, J., Gatherer, A.: Femtocell Networks: A Survey. IEEE Communications Magazine 46(9), 59–67 (2008)
3. Kent, S.: IP Encapsulating Security Payload (ESP). IETF RFC 4303 (2005)
4. Brassil, J., Manadhata, P.K.: Proving the Location of a Mobile Device User. In: 2012 Virgina Tech Wireless Symposium (May 2012)
5. Brassil, J., Manadhata, P.K.: Securing a Femtocell-based Location Service. In: Intl. Conf. on Sel. Areas in Mobile and Wireless Networking (iCOST 2012) (June 2012)
6. Denning, D.E., MacDoran, P.F.: Location-Based Authentication: Grounding Cyberspace for Better Security. In: Computer Fraud & Security (February 1996)
7. Kindberg, T., Zhang, K., Shankar, N.: Context Authentication Using Constrained Channels. In: Proc. of Fourth IEEE WMCSA, pp. 14–21 (2002)
8. Brands, S., Chaum, D.: Distance Bounding Protocols. In: Helleseth, T. (ed.) EUROCRYPT 1993. LNCS, vol. 765, pp. 344–359. Springer, Heidelberg (1994)
9. Luo, W., Hengartner, U.: VeriPlace: A Privacy-Aware Location Proof Architecture. In: Proc. of 18th ACM SIGSPATIAL GIS 2010, pp. 23–32 (2010)
10. Saroiu, S., Wolman, A.: Enabling New Mobile Applications with Location Proofs. In: Proc. of HotMobile 2009, pp. 1–6 (2009)
11. Lenders, V., Koukoumidis, E., Zhang, P., Martonosi, M.: Location-based Trust for Mobile User-Generated Contents: Applications, Challenges and Implementations. In: Proc. of Hotmobile 2008 (2008)
12. Dua, A., Bulusu, N., Hu, W., Feng, W.: Towards Trustworthy Participatory Sensing. In: Proc. of USENIX HotSec (August 2009)
13. Saroiu, S., Wolman, A.: I Am a Sensor, and I Approve This Message. In: Proc. of HotMobile 2010, pp. 37–42 (2010)
14. Gilbert, P., Jung, J., Lee, K., Qin, H., Sharkey, D., Sheth, A., Cox, L.: YouProve: Authenticity and Fidelity in Mobile Sensing. ACM SenSys (2011)
15. Faria, D., Cheriton, D.: No Long-term Secrets: Location Based Security in Overprovisioned Wireless LANs. In: Proc. HotNets-III (2004)
16. Wei, Y., Zeng, K., Mohapatra, P.: Adaptive Wireless Channel Probing for Shared Key Generation. In: Proc. of IEEE Infocom 2011 (2011)
17. Narayanan, A., Thiagarajan, N., Lakhani, M., Hamburg, M., Boneh, D.: Location Privacy via Private Proximity Testing. In: Proc. of NDSS 2011 (2011)
18. Zhang, Y., Li, Z., Trappe, W.: Power-Modulated Challenge-Response Schemes for Verifying Location Claims. In: IEEE Globecom 2007 (2007)
19. Talasila, M., Curtmola, R., Borcea, C.: Location Verification through Immediate Neighbors Knowledge. In: Proc. of Mobiquitous 2010 (2010)
20. Kirkpatrick, M., Bertino, E.: Enforcing Spatial Constraints for Mobile RBAC Systems. In: Proc. SACMAT 2010, pp. 99–108 (2010)
21. Skyhook Wireless, http://www.skyhookwireless.com/
22. Tippenhauer, N., Rasmussen, K., Popper, C., Capkun, S.: Attacks on Public WLAN-based Positioning. In: Proc. of MobiSys 2009 (2009)
23. LOC-AID, Inc., http://www.loc-aid.com

Context-Aware, Data-Driven Policy Enforcement for Smart Mobile Devices in Business Environments

Denis Feth and Christian Jung

Fraunhofer Institute for Experimental Software Engineering IESE,
Fraunhofer-Platz 1, 67663 Kaiserslautern, Germany
{denis.feth,christian.jung}@iese.fraunhofer.de
http://www.iese.fraunhofer.de

Abstract. The popularity of smart mobile devices, initiatives such as "bring your own device", and the increasing overlap of private and business areas are changing the IT landscape and its security requirements. This poses challenges in terms of data security, the adherence to privacy laws, and the protection of business assets. To tackle the problem, we developed a data-driven usage control infrastructure that enables integration of smart mobile devices into business environments. For policy evaluation, our solution comprises the use of fine-grained context information by exploiting the full capabilities of today's mobile devices. The combination of integrated usage control and context awareness promotes the secure application of mobile business apps. In this paper, we present our proof-of-concept implementation and its underlying concepts.

Keywords: IT security, usage control, context-awareness, business integration, Android.

1 Introduction

Nowadays, business applications on smart mobile devices (i.e., smart phones and tablets) are commonplace in many companies. However, the integration of mobile devices poses several challenges in terms of data security and privacy. Most mobile platforms do not provide adequate means for an effective protection of a company's assets, as it is usually the case for classical information systems (e.g., user account management).

In terms of mobile data protection, an important aspect is the management of access permissions. Access control is a well-understood problem, and corresponding access control mechanisms are available in almost any system. However, traditional access control is insufficient for the enforcement of business-critical security policies as it is not possible to put restrictions on the future data usage. For instance, classical access control is not sufficient if an app has access to contacts in general while redistribution of contact information has to be prohibited at the same time.

A.U. Schmidt et al. (Eds.): MOBISEC 2012, LNICST 107, pp. 69–80, 2012.

Enforcing such restrictions is approached by distributed usage control, a generalization of access control [23,26], which enables the enforcement of obligations for future data usage.

In this paper, we focus on the extension of the existing enforcement infrastructure [10] for Android, which is, with an overall market share of more than 52.5 percent [11], the market leading platform for smart phones. Achieving business suitability requires the integration of usage-control-enabled Android devices with existing (enforcement) infrastructures, as well as flexible and context-aware usage policies. The latter enables the specification of policies using additional context information for improving the policy decision process and, subsequently, the policy enforcement. Especially for smart mobile devices this is important, as they are frequently used in varying contexts (e.g., at different locations or in different projects).

Example Scenario. We consider the following scenario to illustrate our work: A company plans to support private smart phones for their managerial staff. Managers synchronize at least their company calendars with their smart phones. However, it cannot be prevented that other data, such as the company address book or business emails, are also synchronized with personal mobile devices. Hence, the company wants to make sure that business information can only be accessed while the manager is in a specific context (e.g., "manager is in a business meeting") and that sensitive data cannot leak from the device. Other usage control examples in this scenario are "anonymize sensitive data before they leave the system", "disable audio recording during meetings", or "pictures taken at the company's premises can only be displayed at work". Sensitive information may include any data stored on the device, such as emails, documents, or photos.

Our scenario illustrates three basic requirements: first, a component that enforces the policies on the device is needed; second, a mechanism to centrally and flexibly deploy policies on all or on one specific device is required; third, a policy language that is highly expressive and allows the definition of abstract contexts such as "manager is working".

Paper structure. In Section 2, we distinguish our work from other related research. In Section 3, we introduce usage control in general, followed by the enforcement infrastructure for Android. Section 4 describes our approach for integrating the enforcement infrastructure into business environments. Context-aware policy evaluation is described in Section 5. Finally, Section 6 summarizes and concludes the work.

2   Related Work

Our work relates to work from the security domain in general, as well as from the areas of usage control, Android security, and context-awareness. In the following, we will give a summary of the most closely related work. Our work differs from all of them in that we explicitly focus on the integration of three parts, namely enforcement of usage control policies on Android, context-awareness and the application in business environments.

Several security extensions for Android have been proposed which differ in the expressiveness of their policy language and the types of policies that can be enforced. Solutions such as MockDroid [5], TISSA [31], Saint [22], CRePE [6], and APEX [20] enable users to deny specific permissions at runtime rather than at installation time. For MockDroid and TISSA, permissions are not denied directly, but faked values are returned for certain API calls, which has benefits in terms of stability of the apps. However, none of these solutions allows an easy and flexible integration into business like our approach. Additionally, our enforcement infrastructure supports more powerful (regarding the monitored events) data-driven policies with complex conditions based on linear temporal logic. Finally, we are able to define and use high level contexts based on various fine-grained input sources (sensors) with our context evaluation engine.

Porscha [21] enforces DRM policies specified in an extension of the OMA REL policy language, including location-based policies. By using identity-based encryption and binding policies to data, Porscha supports business integration as data owners keep control of their data. Our work differs in that we (1) can use less restrictive policies in practice as we support modification of intercepted events instead of inhibition only. Moreover, we have the possibility to define executive actions in our policies. Finally, we consider data flow, and use context information in the policy language.

Like our enforcement infrastructure, the Saint framework [2] uses TaintDroid and data-driven policies supporting context information to prevent the leakage of sensitive data. However, the policy language we use is far more expressive. In contrast to Saint, we can aggregate low-level sensor data for usable and flexible policy specification, and we are not restricted to network-related events.

The ConUCON system [4] is a context-aware adaptation and extension of the UCON model [23] for Android. It allows the enforcement of temporal or spatial constraints or system properties before and during events. To a certain extend, the framework is comparable to our work. However, we take data flow and context information into account. Furthermore, we use OSL for policy specification which enables more sophisticated policies.

There exist several frameworks for enhancing Android with context-awareness, such as ContextDroid [27], CAMF (Context-aware Machine Learning Framework) [29], fünf [18] or ContextProvider [19]. All these frameworks provide context information mainly for apps. In contrast to our solution that is directly integrated into the Android Application Framework, they run as user applications, which is detrimental in terms of security. Moreover, our solution aggregates low-level sensor data to high-level context information, based on flexible context configuration expressions.

Apart from Android enforcement [10], there exist usage control implementations for OpenBSD [12], X11 [25], Java [7,14], machine languages [9,30] and dedicated applications such as Thunderbird [16] and social networks [15], as well as in the context of digital rights management [1,17]. Compared to our work, these implementations mainly differ in the abstraction level, and do neither include context-awareness nor allow an easy integration into business environments.

3   Policy Enforcement for Android

In this section, we introduce fundamental usage control concepts and outline the current enforcement infrastructure for Android as introduced in [10].

Usage Control. Usage control [23,26] is a generalization of access control. It puts obligations on the use of data that specify what must or must not happen to data after access to it has been granted. Common usage control implementations contain at least three components: a Policy Enforcement Point (PEP), a Policy Decision Point (PDP), and a Policy Information Point (PIP). The PEP is responsible for intercepting relevant events and for enforcing the deployed policies by either allowing, inhibiting, or modifying the intercepted event (see below). Policy evaluation is done by the PDP, which decides whether a certain event is allowed or not. For this decision, it might consult a PIP, which provides additional information not contained in the event, such as information on context or data flow. The consideration of data flow enables the specification of representation-independent policies. Representation-independence means that not only the original data representation (e.g., a certain file) is protected, but all its manifestations and duplicates (e.g., all files, caches, or screens containing data from the original file).

Our usage control policies are specified in XML and are based on the Obligation Specification Language (OSL) [13]. They contain a set of ECA-rules (event-condition-action), each describing a trigger event, a condition in OSL (e.g., "at most three times"), and an action that has to be executed if the condition is satisfied. Our system supports four different enforcement types. Suppose, for example, that we want to enforce "no personal data is allowed to leave the system" on a message-passing interface with a firewall-like component, we have the following enforcement options:

- *No enforcement*: The message is allowed without further modification. As this is the standard case, our enforcement framework works similar to a firewall with a blacklist approach.
- *Enforcement by inhibition*: The message is rejected or simply dropped.
- *Enforcement by modification*: Message fields are modified (e.g., anonymized).
- *Enforcement by execution*: Additional actions, such as sending a notification message to the system administrator, are executed.

Android Architecture. Android is built of several layers including the operating system, middleware, and a set of key applications. It is based on a Linux kernel that provides hardware abstraction and other basic functionalities to the upper layers such as process, memory, and power management as well as networking and basic security mechanisms.

The Android system core (application framework) is written in Java and runs in the Dalvik Virtual Machine (DVM), a Java virtual machine for Android's bytecode format 'dex'. The application framework provides both APIs for application developers and several core services (e.g., location services) running within the system process.

Android apps are Java programs that are composed of activities (UI screens), services, broadcast receivers and content providers. The three first-named component types are invoked via so-called intents (Android specific messages). Content providers are used to share data among apps via SQL-like interfaces.

In terms of security, the operating system provides basic discretionary access control (DAC). Each installed app has its own user and group ID, so that access to the file system and privileged operations can be controlled by the kernel. Furthermore, Android uses a special permission system that regulates access to resources on a higher level. At development time, an app's author has to explicitly declare in the app's manifest file required permissions that are checked in the application framework at runtime. Similar to traditional access control, it is not possible to protect resources once a permission has been granted.

Usage Control on Android. To implement usage control on Android, a reference monitor enforces usage control policies at the Application Framework level. This is a fundamental decision, as the choice of the abstraction layer determinates the type of policies that can be enforced. The monitor is implemented as a system service that monitors intents, permission requests (e.g., whether an app has permission to access the Internet), queries to content providers (in order to access private data of another app) and certain events that are relevant in terms of data flow (e.g., network traffic). This reference monitor is controlled via the *Security Manager* app, which also provides the user interface and means for policy management. To enable representation-independent policies, TaintDroid [8] is used for tracking data flows (see Section 5).

4   Business Integration

The current implementation of our enforcement infrastructure enforces flexible, data-driven policies on Android devices, but it still lacks some properties that are necessary for an integrated business solution. First, usage control is currently enforced only locally on the device. There are no means to send confidential data to the device while protecting the data through automatic deployment of usage control policies. In the opposite direction, protected content is not secured when leaving the device. However, this is mandatory for an effective protection of business assets as business apps usually exchange data with backend systems. Second, as smart mobile devices are used in varying contexts (e.g., at different locations or in different projects) and there is a trend to use private devices also in business (BYOD) [3], there is a need for flexible context-aware policy evaluation. As the overlap between private and business use-cases is increasing steadily [24], context-awareness is particularly important. We will cover this topic in Section 5.

4.1   Architecture

For an integrated business solution, the current enforcement infrastructure has
to be changed in a way that allows the integration of a usage-control-enabled
device into an overall context. If a data provider (sender) wants to send sensitive
data to the mobile device (data in transit), the provider needs to ensure that the
corresponding policy is deployed on the target device. Technically, this can be
achieved in two ways. The sender could encrypt the data and directly attach the
policy to the data item. Alternatively, the sender can deploy the policy manually
before releasing sensitive data. We chose the latter option, as neither a continuous
monitoring of network traffic (unfavorable with respect to performance) nor the
use of encryption and a special data container format is required. Therefore, we
need to provide suitable interfaces for remote policy deployment on the device.

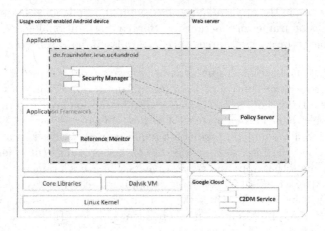

Fig. 1. Deployment

Figure 1 shows the high level deployment in our system that contains three
basic actors: A set of Android devices, a central policy server and the C2DM
(Cloud to Device Messaging) service provided by Google. The enforcement infrastructure is indicated by the gray box.

As depicted earlier, the reference monitor enforces local policies by monitoring intents, content provider requests, permission checks, and certain data sinks
[10]. The Security Manager app provides the user interface for the policy enforcement system, and it manages all remote connections to the policy server. It also
implements the storage and management of policies. Finally, the policy server
provides means to deploy policies on remote devices without directly communicating to them. The deployment procedure may also include the negotiation of
common data identifiers that allow the system-wide identification of data and
are needed for the proper specification of policies.

To initiate the communication with the server, we use the Google C2DM
service. This setting has several benefits:

- The system does not need to maintain a permanent, active data connection. Instead, we send a push notification whenever a policy needs to be deployed. The device can then contact the policy server to fetch the policy.
- A centralized policy server is easier to maintain and provides a central point for communication. For example, exceptions can be handled directly by the policy server (e.g., if a device is not available) and policies can easily be deployed in parallel on multiple registered devices of the domain.

However, a centralized architecture has also some disadvantages that need to be addressed:

- The server may become a bottleneck or a central point for attacks. However, if the policy server goes offline (e.g., due to a DoS attack), there is no risk for the data provider to leak sensitive data. As he knows that a certain policy could not be deployed, he can simply not release the sensitive data.
- Using C2DM means relying on third-party services. However, this is not critical because (1) we do not send sensitive data (including policies) via these services and (2) it is possible to change this model and to implement a solution without these services (while accepting the negative effect on battery power).
  Moreover, C2DM requires a Google account on each smart phone, which we assume to be fulfilled anyway, as it is necessary for productive use (e.g., for using the Play Store).
- Both policy server and mobile device require an Internet connection to use C2DM. However, we assume that this requirement is met in most cases, especially in business environments.

4.2   Policy Deployment in Business Environments

Due to space limitations, we omit a detailed architecture description but show the policy deployment procedure to illustrate on the runtime behavior. Figure 2 shows how a data provider can deploy policies to devices. The complete communication is protected via TLS/SSL. We assume a public key infrastructure (PKI) to ensure a proper mutual authentication and transport encryption between the communication partners (i.e., the Security Manager on the target device and the remote data/policy provider). We refer to [10] for a security analysis for the enforcement framework. For the remote policy deployment, we rely on the security and reliability of the TLS/SSL protocol and the external PKI.

In the first step, the provider sends the policy to the policy server and requests the deployment to a certain target device that is registered at the server. Via C2DM, the server sends a push notification to the target device and triggers the deployment process. The target device fetches the policy (which is not included in the C2DM notification for security reasons) from the server and tries to deploy it. If the deployment succeeds, the sender is notified by the server. As the sender can rely on the correct policy deployment, the sensitive data can be sent to the device.

Another important aspect in business environments is the integration into the data flow model of the overall context. As we use TaintDroid for local data flow

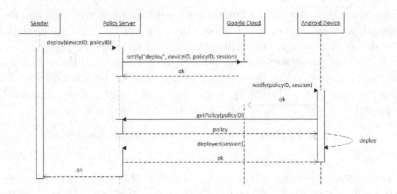

Fig. 2. Sequence diagram showing policy deployment

tracking, we have to provide a mapping between global data IDs and internal taint markings. The mapping procedure is realized similarly to the policy deployment. The data provider requests a taint marking for an initial data representation via the policy server. To this end, the sender provides a provider-specific data ID matching a certain data item. The policy server will forward this request to the device, which creates a mapping between the given data ID and a free, local taint marking. After this taint mark has been returned to the sender, the data provider can use it to specify policies that are representation-independent in the global system including the smart mobile device. An important drawback of TaintDroid is the amount of available taint markings, which is currently limited to 32. This is sufficient for our proof-of-concept, but an open issue for productive use.

5   Extending the Solution with a Context-Aware PIP

Our enforcement approach is currently event-based and uses **only** data that is contained in the event for decision making. Hence, all needed information has to be collected and included in the request from the PEP to the PDP. Obviously, this entails two main disadvantages:

First, the PEP needs to obtain additional information that has to be added to the event for decision making. As a result, we have to use the events for keeping the internal PDP state up-to-date. Second, all information is processed in one central component, the PDP, turning it into a potential bottleneck and aggravating the need for real time capability. Apart from this, the PDP has to understand the provided information, which increases its complexity. This is especially critical for complex information, such as context data.

As a consequence, we have to introduce external components that interact with the PDP for collecting and processing relevant context information. In the literature, such components are known as Policy Information Points (PIPs) [28]. These PIPs relief the PDP of sophisticated context elicitation and assessment operations, and provide the required information through a dedicated interface.

In our scenario, we demand the control of company related information and the prevention of uncontrolled data leakage. Thus, we have to control, but also to track, information flow in the system. To this end, we use an information-flow tracking system, called TaintDroid, as mentioned above. TaintDroid's basic approach is to assign a specific mark, a so-called taint tag, to certain data fragments. These tags are stored along with the data in a modified version of the Dalvik memory stack. On each data operation, the operands' tags are combined and maintained even across process boundaries. For example, copying a file (or parts of a file) into a new file results in copying the data together with the embedded taint tags, thus tainting the new file with the origin's taint tags. Using TaintDroid with a special usage control tainting, we obtain a PIP providing information on the information flow, which enables us to enforce representation-independent, data-driven policies.

Apart from data flow control, our enforcement framework also supports context-aware policies depending on the current situation of the user. To this end, we developed a so-called *Context Manager* for collecting and processing system and context information. The Context Manager aggregates and evaluates raw data collected by various context sensors to provide high-level context information, which can directly be referenced by the PDP for decision making.

The Context Manager consists of three layers, as shown in Figure 3. The lowest layer is the *sensor layer*. This layer provides several sensor implementations that are responsible for collecting raw context data from the system. We currently have a location sensor to retrieve configurable location information (e.g., minimum change in location), as well as an accelerometer, a battery, a Bluetooth, a settings and a WiFi sensor. Furthermore, we implemented a calendar sensor, which retrieves calendar-related data such as "free", "busy", "tentative", or "out of office".

All active sensors pass their data to the next layer, the *data layer*. This layer has two main responsibilities. First, it stores all sensor data in a suitable format, including timestamps. Second, it schedules the appropriate sensors as required by the context specifications that need to be monitored on behalf of the policy specifications. One parameter affecting the scheduling is the age of sensor data.

The next layer, the *evaluation layer*, has an evaluation engine and several evaluators. The evaluators request preformatted data from the *data layer* to derive abstract, high-level notions of contexts. The evaluators return values that are compared in a so-called comparator mechanisms (i.e., equals, greater than, lower than), which results in a Boolean value. Finally, the evaluation engine logically combines the results from the comparator mechanisms. This is done when (1) the PDP calls the Context Manager or (2) the data layer pushes new data.

Relying on the Context Manager, policies can refer to high-level context conditions such as "manager is on a business trip", "manager is at home" or "manager is working". The Context Manager translates these notions into low-level context data readings such as locations, network connectivity, and user interactions. To decide on a context-dependent policy, the PDP consults the Context Manager, without having deeper knowledge of the context itself.

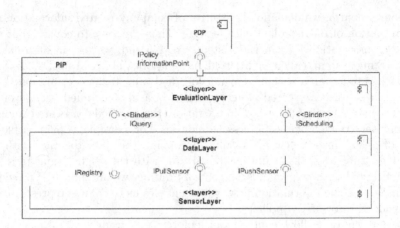

Fig. 3. Context Manager Architecture

To a certain extent, mobile business applications rely on information from their backend systems where all distributed information is gathered. Our approach is flexible enough to leverage such backend information by integrating the backends as additional PIP or context sensors. However, such an integration may sometimes be prohibitive in terms of response-time constraints.

In summary, we can specify sophisticated usage control policies that use additional information from integrated (e.g., TaintDroid, Context Manager) or external (e.g., backend systems) PIPs.

6   Conclusion and Future Work

In response to the emerging need for mobile data protection in business, we have developed an approach for the integration of a context-aware adaptation of the Android usage control enforcement infrastructure[10] into business environments. Using a central policy server, policies can easily be managed and deployed on mobile devices by the providers of sensitive data or by IT security administrators. As performance is a key factor for the acceptance of security solutions, we decided to use and push services and non-sticky policies that do not require data encryption to optimize energy consumption.

As modern mobile workers frequently change context, and private and business contexts increasingly overlap, flexible runtime adaptations of policies are necessary. We tackle this problem by our multi-layered Context Manager that aggregates low-level sensor data and provides high-level context information (such as "manager is working"), which can be referenced in policies as high-level context conditions. By doing so, we can exploit the full potential of smart mobile devices on the one hand and ease the specification of policies on the other.

For business integration, the current amount of available taint marks is insufficient and has to be increased. Future work will investigate appropriate solutions for this issue.

Also, the usable and intuitive specification of policies is one of our current research topics. The current formalisms for usage control policies are very low-level and require experts for policy specification. Since this is not appropriate even in business environments, we research methods to enable ordinary users to specify security policies in a simple and understandable way.

Finally, we will investigate the role of the context manager in enhancing user experience and in increasing productivity of mobile workers by automatically selecting appropriate security-related system settings without user intervention, based on the situational context of the user.

References

1. Adobe LiveCycle Rights Management ES (August 2010),
   http://www.adobe.com/products/livecycle/rightsmanagement/indepth.html
2. Ahmed, M., Ahamad, M.: Protecting health information on mobile devices. In: CODASPY 2012: Proceedings of the Second ACM Conference on Data and Application Security and Privacy (2012)
3. Aruba Networks Inc. Byod adoption is growing amongst emea enterprises, despite security concerns; survey shows (May 2012),
   http://www.arubanetworks.com/news-releases/byod-adoption-is-growing/
4. Bai, G., Gu, L., Feng, T., Guo, Y., Chen, X.: Context-Aware Usage Control for Android. In: Jajodia, S., Zhou, J. (eds.) SecureComm 2010. LNICST, vol. 50, pp. 326–343. Springer, Heidelberg (2010)
5. Beresford, A., Rice, A., Skehin, N.: Mockdroid: trading privacy for application functionality on smartphones. In: Proc. 12th Workshop on Mobile Computing Systems and Applications (2011)
6. Conti, M., Nguyen, V.T.N., Crispo, B.: CRePE: context-related policy enforcement for android, pp. 331–345 (October 2010)
7. Dam, M., Jacobs, B., Lundblad, A., Piessens, F.: Security Monitor Inlining for Multithreaded Java. In: Drossopoulou, S. (ed.) ECOOP 2009. LNCS, vol. 5653, pp. 546–569. Springer, Heidelberg (2009)
8. Enck, W., Gilbert, P., Chun, B., Cox, L., Jung, J., McDaniel, P., Sheth, A.: Taintdroid: An information-flow tracking system for realtime privacy monitoring on smartphones. In: Proc. 9th USENIX Symposium on Operating Systems Design and Implementation (2010)
9. Erlingsson, U., Schneider, F.: SASI enforcement of security policies: A retrospective. In: Proc. New Security Paradigms Workshop, pp. 87–95 (1999)
10. Feth, D., Pretschner, A.: Flexible Data-Driven Security for Android. In: SERE 2012: Proceedings of the sixth International Conference on Software Security and Reliability. IEEE (to appear, 2012)
11. Gartner: Gartner Says Sales of Mobile Devices Grew 5.6 Percent in Third Quarter of 2011; Smartphone Sales Increased 42 Percent (November 2011),
    http://www.gartner.com/it/page.jsp?id=1848514
12. Harvan, M., Pretschner, A.: State-based Usage Control Enforcement with Data Flow Tracking using System Call Interposition. In: Proc. 3rd Intl. Conf. on Network and System Security, pp. 373–380 (2009)
13. Hilty, M., Pretschner, A., Basin, D., Schaefer, C., Walter, T.: A Policy Language for Distributed Usage Control. In: Biskup, J., López, J. (eds.) ESORICS 2007. LNCS, vol. 4734, pp. 531–546. Springer, Heidelberg (2007)

14. Ion, I., Dragovic, B., Crispo, B.: Extending the Java Virtual Machine to Enforce Fine-Grained Security Policies in Mobile Devices. In: Proc. Annual Computer Security Applications Conference, pp. 233–242. IEEE Computer Society (2007)

15. Kumari, P., Pretschner, A., Peschla, J., Kuhn, J.-M.: Distributed data usage control for web applications: a social network implementation. In: Proceedings of the First ACM Conference on Data and Application Security and Privacy, CODASPY 2011, pp. 85–96 (2011)

16. Lörscher, M.: Usage control for a mail client. Master's thesis, University of Kaiserslautern (February 2012)

17. Microsoft. Windows Rights Management Services (2010), http://www.microsoft.com/windowsserver2008/en/us/ad-rms-overview.aspx

18. MIT Media Labs. fünf Open Sensing Framework (2010)

19. Mitchell, M., Meyers, C., Wang, A.-I.A., Tyson, G.: Contextprovider: Context awareness for medical monitoring applications. In: Proceedings of the 33rd Annual International Conference of the IEEE Engineering in Medicine and Biology Society, EMBC (2011)

20. Nauman, M., Khan, S.: Design and implementation of a fine-grained resource usage model for the android platform (2010)

21. Ongtang, M., Butler, K., McDaniel, P.: Porscha: policy oriented secure content handling in android. In: Proceedings of the 26th Annual Computer Security Applications Conference, ACSAC 2010, pp. 221–230. ACM, New York (2010)

22. Ongtang, M., McLaughlin, S., Enck, W., McDaniel, P.: Semantically rich application-centric security in android. In: Annual Computer Security Applications Conference, ACSAC 2009, pp. 340–349 (December 2009)

23. Park, J., Sandhu, R.: The UCON ABC usage control model. ACM Trans. Inf. Syst. Secur. 7(1), 128–174 (2004)

24. Power, R., Cranor, L., Farb, M., Jackson, C., Goldschlag, D., Griss, M., Cristin, N., Joshi, S., Perrig, A., Tague, P., Tude, E., Mistretta, M.: Mobility and Security. Dazzling Opportunities, Profound Challenges. Technical report, McAfee (2011)

25. Pretschner, A., Buechler, M., Harvan, M., Schaefer, C., Walter, T.: Usage control enforcement with data flow tracking for x11. In: Proc. 5th Intl. Workshop on Security and Trust Management, pp. 124–137 (2009)

26. Pretschner, A., Hilty, M., Basin, D.: Distributed usage control. Commun. ACM 49(9), 39–44 (2006)

27. van Wissen, B., Palmer, N., Kemp, R., Kielmann, T., Bal, H.: ContextDroid: an expression-based context framework for Android. In: Proceedings of PhoneSense 2010 (November 2010)

28. Vollbrecht, J., Calhoun, P., Farrell, S., Gommans, L., Gross, G., de Bruijn, B., de Laat, C., Holdrege, M., Spence, D.: Aaa authorization framework (August 2000), http://tools.ietf.org/html/rfc2904

29. Wang, A.I., Ahmad, Q.K.: Camf context-aware machine learning framework for android. Science And Technology (2010)

30. Yee, B., Sehr, D., Dardyk, G., Chen, J., Muth, R., Ormandy, T., Okasaka, S., Narula, N., Fullagar, N.: Native Client: A Sandbox for Portable, Untrusted x86 Native Code. In: Proc IEEE Symposium on Security and Privacy, pp. 79–93 (2009)

31. Zhou, Y., Zhang, X., Jiang, X., Freeh, V.W.: Taming Information-Stealing Smartphone Applications (on Android). In: McCune, J.M., Balacheff, B., Perrig, A., Sadeghi, A.-R., Sasse, A., Beres, Y. (eds.) Trust 2011. LNCS, vol. 6740, pp. 93–107. Springer, Heidelberg (2011)

Securing Mobile Device-Based Machine Interactions with User Location Histories

Philipp Marcus, Moritz Kessel, and Claudia Linnhoff-Popien

Ludwig Maximilian University of Munich,
Mobile and Distributed Systems Group,
Oettingenstr. 67, 80538 Munich, Germany
{philipp.marcus,moritz.kessel,linnhoff}@ifi.lmu.de

Abstract. Mobile devices are more and more integrated in workflows, especially when interacting with stationary resources like machines in order to improve productivity or usability, but risk unauthorized access or unwanted unattended operation. Systems for location based access control have been developed to restrict the user to be in specific locations in order to proceed in a workflow. However, these approaches do not consider the movement pattern of a user nor do they distinguish the severity of false-positives that might arise from imperfect location measurements which is crucial in certain workflows. In this paper, focusing on mobile users interacting with stationary machines, an approach for workflow policies is presented using three types of location constraints to enforce movement patterns. The evaluation of these constraints is based on a user's location history which is generated in a tamper-proof environment on his mobile device and describes his geographical trajectory for a given timespan.

Keywords: Location Based Access Control, Movement Patterns, Location Histories, Mobile Workflows, Location Constraints.

1 Introduction

How can the productivity of users and the usability of static objects and resources like machines be increased? One step in this direction is to provide access over a standardized interface using mobile devices. From this mobilization, often a security problem arises when mobile devices are allowed to be at any geographical location while interacting with static security relevant objects and resources. The controlled re-coupling of possible actions to specific geographical locations is realized by systems for location based access control. In the last years, many approaches for security models have been developed that restrict the mobile execution of actions on predefined objects to specific locations using location constraints. The uncertainty of a user's location has been dealt with by introducing lower bounds for the probability that a location constraint is satisfied, partially allowing false-positive access permissions. More specialized policies have been developed in the context of workflows. Here, as a possibility

A.U. Schmidt et al. (Eds.): MOBISEC 2012, LNICST 107, pp. 81–92, 2012.
© Institute for Computer Sciences, Social Informatics and Telecommunications Engineering 2012

to improve productivity and security at the same time, workflow management systems (WfMS) have been designed that make only those actions available to a user that are relevant for the current progress or state of a workflow based on the geographical location of the user.

However, existing approaches for WfMS and workflow definitions with location based access control do not allow to constrain the set of possible subsequent actions for a given action based on a user's movement pattern during the execution of the action, i.e., the exact geographical trajectory the user has covered. Furthermore existing approaches lack the possibility to differentiate between the severity of several false-positives and to limit it to an upper bound. This especially becomes a problem, when special policies need to be expressed, e.g., for workflows where it is crucial for the duration of an action that a user stays within a given location, i.e., due to hygiene regulations, or walks along a given sequence of locations, e.g., to ensure his focus on relevant physical aspects.

In this paper, a new approach for workflow policies is presented, based on location histories of users to enforce movement patterns in workflows focusing on actions on machines. A WfMS, called *abstract machine* has been developed, which accepts *mobile action requests* from a mobile device executing a given workflow, checks if they conform to a given workflow policy and is able to translate requests to input signals for machines. Location constraints have been developed, that allow policies to require movement patterns during two mobile action requests like the continuous attendance of a user in an exactly defined region, called *logical location*, or the migration along a given sequence of logical locations. An abstract machine is able to intercept *invalid* mobile action requests if they violate the predefined workflow or its policy, reducing the possibility of unwanted or flawed results. This allows the adherence to specific security and quality regulations.

The rest of the paper is structured as follows: Section 2 first introduces our adversary model. Section 3 presents the notion of workflows and the developed system architecture, followed by the developed security model. This model is described in detail along with the developed location constraints for abidance, containment and migration. Section 4 illustrates the expressiveness of the developed workflow policy model in an example scenario. Related work is presented in Section 5 and finally, Section 6 concludes the paper and outlines research directions for future work.

2   The Adversary Model

The system has been designed to cope with the implications of an adversary model, which is presented in this section. It outlines how a potential adversary could attack the defined system. An adversary is able to pick up lost devices of all users and even to steal them. If an adversary takes control of another user's device he is not able to pretend that user's identity due to a sufficient authentication scheme. If he uses a device he can deposit it while moving around, and thus pretending a wrong geographical trajectory if the device' location is assumed to be the user's location, too.

On the other hand, the adversary is only able to manipulate mobile devices. That way he is not able to manipulate installed positioning infrastructure, for example GPS, to conduct faked location measurements, as only such infrastructure is employed, which allows no or at least very costly attacks. This even prevents the adversary from disturbing other users from conducting valid measurements by installing disturbing sources. Furthermore we assume, that a mobile device prevents an adversary from manipulating it to pretend to be in a given location or to generate random timestamps, as all employed mobile devices are equipped with trusted computing capabilities which allow the attestation that no system components have been modified or compromised.

3   Securing Mobile Device-Based Machine Interactions

Machine interaction using mobile devices has been modeled using workflows with policies which are both presented in this section.

3.1   Describing Machine Interaction as Workflows

The set of possible sequences of actions invoked by mobile devices on machines can be restricted by defining a set of workflows, i.e., describing reasonable sequences of actions.

The developed concept of workflow policies based on movement patterns is presented using an abstract workflow specification language. Hereby, in line with typical workflow specification languages [1,2], we define a workflow $w = (\mathcal{A}, \to_{\mathcal{A}})$ on a set of actions $\mathcal{A}$ along with a causal relationship $\to_{\mathcal{A}}$ which describes for each pair of actions $a, a' \in \mathcal{A}$, if a' is an allowed subsequent action of a. Transitions between actions with respect to $\to_{\mathcal{A}}$ are assumed to be atomic. Single actions of $\mathcal{A}$ may correspond to interactions with machines. Each workflow starts with an initial action •, ends with a final action ○ and can contain transitions to an abort action ⊗, which are all elements of $\mathcal{A}$ for every workflow. The set of all workflows is denoted as $\mathcal{W}$. Extensions with more expressive techniques for workflow definition are not within the scope of this paper.

A system architecture has been developed that allows a mobile user to proceed in a workflow from an action a to an action a', if he sends a *mobile action request* that is granted and is referring a' and his last granted request a. The developed system architecture is presented in detail in the next section.

3.2   System Architecture

A system architecture has been developed that realizes mobile device based access to machines using a mediator to enforce access confirming to a defined workflow and a policy that is based on users' movement patterns. It generally consists of three entities: Mobile devices, machines and abstract machines. An architectural overview is depicted in Figure 1. Machines represent physically

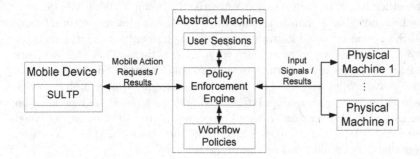

Fig. 1. The developed system architecture for mobile machine interaction: abstract machines mediate mobile action requests to machines

existing machines or devices that are needed to complete single actions of workflows. Abstract machines incorporate a WfMS: To communicate with a physical machine, mobile users send *mobile action requests* to the mediating abstract machine $\widetilde{am}$ which is defined for a given set of workflows $\mathcal{W}$ and workflow policies, which are explained in detail in Section 3.3. Finally an authorization decision is taken by the *policy enforcement engine* and corresponding input signals are sent by $\widetilde{am}$ to the machine referred by the action the request refers to. Possible results are then returned to the user.

A security model has been defined, that assigns each user a set of roles and each role a set of workflows with their corresponding policies. When a user logs in at the abstract machine with a username and selects a role that is available to him, he is provided a set of available workflows and chooses a workflow w from this set. Before the execution of w starts, a new *user session* is created within the abstract machine, which is explained in more detail later in this section.

Collecting Samples of Trajectories. The movement pattern of a user is defined as the exact geographical trajectory he has covered during the execution of an action of a workflow. To capture this trajectory with a user's device, a software component called *secure user location token provider* (*sultp*) has been designed which collects samples of the trajectory and runs on the mobile device D of each user. For each sample a *secure user location token* is created. A secure user location token t describes the location l of the device D for a given point of time *time* using a probability density function *pdf*. Due to varying environmental influences, positioning systems are inherently subject to errors which only allows to describe measured locations with a certain probability distribution specific to the used technology [3]. For the rest of this paper, a *sultp* is assumed to sample movement patterns as pdfs using GPS, which allows a description of the error distribution with a bivariate gaussian normal distribution [4].

Furthermore the identity u of the user currently holding a mobile device is included in the secure user location token and detected using an implicit and continuous user authentication like SenGuard developed by Shi et al. [5]. This prevents an adversary from depositing his mobile device or passing it to someone else thereby preventing it from capturing the adversary's real movement pattern. As already mentioned in Section 2, each mobile user is assumed to have a mobile device that employs trusted computing technologies, e.g., by using mobile trusted modules. This allows a mobile device to generate an *attest* that can be verified by an abstract machine, proving that security relevant software components including device drivers, the OS stack and the *sultp* have valid integrity and been loaded correctly. This prohibits an adversary from manipulating the collected samples of trajectories, e.g., by installing malware on the device. Furthermore, the internal clocks of each mobile device are tamper-proof and synchronized to the clock of the abstract machine which prevents an adversary from generating incorrect tokens by manipulating a device's clock. A secure user location token provider is assigned a public-private-key pair K_D^+, K_D^- at the time of its installation, whereby the private key can be stored using the mobile trusted module [6]. Formally, a secure user location token t has been defined as the digital signature of $\langle pdf, time, u, attest \rangle$ with the private key K_D^- of the device. Given a token t, the access to single components is written using $t.pdf$, $t.time$ and so on. In the rest of the paper, $\tau(t)$ abbreviates the notation $t.time$.

A *location history* h is a representation of a users movement pattern consisting of a sequence of chronologically ordered secure user location tokens, $h = \langle t_0, \ldots, t_n \rangle$ having $\forall i \in \{0, \ldots, n-1\} : \tau(t_i) < \tau(t_{i+1})$.

Mobile Action Requests. A mobile action request r has the form $\langle a, h \rangle$ with $a \in \mathcal{A}$ for a workflow $(\mathcal{A}, \rightarrow_{\mathcal{A}}) \in \mathcal{W}$ and with a *location history* $h = \langle t_0, \ldots, t_n \rangle$ consisting of at least one *secure user location token*.

User Sessions. A user u can execute one workflow at once which is handled in the context of a user session $(u, w, t_{last}, a_{last}, timestamp_a)$ with $w \in \mathcal{W}$ and parameters from his last granted action request $r_{last} = (a_{last}, \langle t_0, \ldots, t_{last} \rangle)$ and $timestamp_a$ denoting the timestamp when r_{last} was received by the abstract machine. All, t_{last}, a_{last} and $timestamp_a$ are assigned to $\perp$ if the user has not yet triggered an action request in this session. For a given user u, $s(u)$ denotes his corresponding session. The principle of recording a location history between the activation of an action a and a mobile action request r_i is depicted in Figure 2. The location history of a mobile action requests $r = (a, h = \langle t_0, \ldots, t_n \rangle)$ is called *valid* in the context of a session $s(u)$, if the oldest location token t_0 in h is newer than the last received user location token $s(u).t_{last}$, i.e., $\tau(t_0) > \tau(s(u).t_{last})$ or $s(u).t_{last} = \perp$. Otherwise the mobile action request is immediately denied by $\widetilde{am}$.

3.3   A Security Model Based on Movement Patterns

A workflow policy model has been developed, that allows to further restrict transitions $a \rightarrow_{\mathcal{A}} a'$ of a workflow w by additionally introducing constraints on the location histories of users. Therefore, a policy $\mathcal{P}(w)$ is defined for each workflow and consists of *interaction rules*: $\langle a, a', location\text{-}constraint \rangle$ specifying

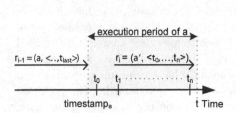 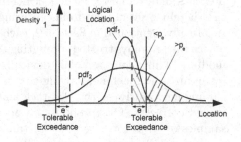

Fig. 2. A location history $t_0, \ldots, t_n$ is recorded between two mobile action requests r_{i-1}, r_i as a sequence of secure user location tokens

Fig. 3. Using measurements with low accuracies, constraining the tolerable exceedance decreases the part of logical locations where a user can be assumed to be within

for a given user u that an action request $r = \langle a', h \rangle$ is granted if the last triggered action of u was a and h satisfies the *location-constraint*.

The Concept of Location Constraints. A location constraint is defined as a predicate which is evaluated by an abstract machine's policy enforcement engine in the context of a user session each time a mobile action request with a valid location history h arrives and is defined as `true` if h conforms to predefined geographical trajectories with a certain probability. Three kinds of location constraints have been developed: abidance, containment and migration constraints which are explained in detail later in this section. These constraints intend to restrict a user's movement pattern and are evaluated based on the user's location history $h = \langle t_0, \ldots, t_n \rangle$, i.e., his sampled movement pattern. Therefore, for the definition of location constraints an approximation of possible geographical trajectories of a user between two such samples t_i and t_{i+1} needs to be inferred. This is accomplished with a function $f(t.pdf, age)$ which predicts a new pdf describing the user location for the time $\tau(t) + age$ with age being an arbitrary timespan describing the age of t. Internally, f can be defined as a convolution of $t.pdf$ with a probability distribution describing the possible user movement in time age with a maximum speed of $v_{\max}$.

To express location constraints, the security model additionally holds a set $\mathcal{L}$ specifying a set of *logical locations*: A logical location l is defined as a tuple $l = (T, id)$ with T being a compact subset of $\mathbb{R}^2$ forming a polygon which represents its extent and id representing a set of human-readable identifiers. Given a logical location l, access to T or id is written as $l.T$ or $l.id$.

Quality Aspects in Location Constraints. When constraining a user's movement pattern in a workflow policy to be completely within a location l, the pdf of each token of the users location history needs to imply that the user was in l with a minimum probability p at the time the measurement has been taken. To exclude cases where a possible adversary could leave l between two measurements and fool the system of being permanently in l, the containment in l needs to be checked for the complete timespan between the creation of two tokens. This is accomplished by generating pdfs from each token t using the previously defined function $f(t.pdf, age)$ which incorporates the possible user movement during the time age since the token has been created. Overall, given a token t with age age, it is checked that a user has not left a location l since t has been created using $t.pdf$ by checking if $p \leq \int_{l.T} f(t.pdf, age)$ evaluates to **true**. In the worst case, this leaves an uncertainty that the user is outside of l after time age which is limited by an upper bound of $1 - p$ and thus also restricts the probability of leaving and reentering l.

If a user's token fulfills this constraint though the user is actually outside of l, the severity of the false-positive decision, i.e., the geographical distance from l, needs to be bounded. Hence, also a tolerable exceedance e along with the probability p_e is specified that additionally constrains acceptable measurements to those where the probability that the user is further than e away from l is maximal p_e. Let $expand : \mathbb{R}^2 \times \mathbb{R} \mapsto \mathbb{R}^2$ be a function expanding a connected area by e, a measured pdf in a token t needs to satisfy $p_e \geq 1 - \int_{expand(l.T,e)} f(t.pdf, age)$.

Example: Consider two collected samples pdf_1 and pdf_2 of the trajectory of a user's device which have a very different covariance, each representing the position of the device at the point of time the corresponding measurement has been taken. This is depicted in Figure 3 for the one-dimensional case. Though for each of the two pdfs the probability that the device is within the depicted logical location may satisfy a defined lower bound of p, both pdfs allow a user to be outside the location with a probability of $1 - p$ but pdf_2 implies a much higher probability that the device is actually much farther away from the location than pdf_1. Defining a tolerable exceedance e together with p_e filters out low-accuracy measurements like pdf_2 and simultaneously limits the severity of possible errors to a maximum of e with high probability.

Definition of Location Constraints. Three different location constraints have been defined restricting the location or the movement pattern of the user to a certain area, possibly consisting of multiple logical locations.

The most basic constraint is the abidance constraint ac which constrains a user u to be in a logical location $l \in \mathcal{L}$ at the point of time ts when a mobile action request $r = (a, \langle t_0, \ldots, t_n \rangle)$ is evaluated. Conform to the assumption that the user's position is modeled as a pdf, a minimum probability p of being in l and a tolerable exceedance e along with a probability p_e is defined as discussed above. The constraint is evaluated for the location history $\langle t_0, \ldots, t_n \rangle$ of u and includes the spreading of the pdf with the previously defined function f for the elapsed timespan $ts - \tau(t_n)$ since the last location token t_n in the location history was generated. An abidance constraint is defined as:

$$ac(l, p, e, p_e, \langle t_0, \ldots, t_n \rangle, ts) \Leftrightarrow p \leq \int_{l.T} f(t_n.pdf, ts - \tau(t_n))$$

$$\wedge \; p_e \geq 1 - \int_{expand(l.T,e)} f(t_n.pdf, ts - \tau(t_n)) \quad (1)$$

Here, the use of f prevents an adversary from fooling the system by sending an old t_n that does not reflect his position at the point of time ts when ac is evaluated. Note that constraining the tolerable exceedance using e and p_e could also be achieved with a second ac on $expand(l.T, e)$. Also note that abidance constraints are the only constraints that utilize only a part of the location history (i.e., the last token) for the evaluation.

With a containment constraint cc, the movement pattern of a user till a point in time ts is constrained to be completely contained within a single logical location l. Since actual movement pattern of a user might be a trajectory that leaves and reenters l which could be undetected if only the collected tokens of his location history were examined (due to the allowed irregular collection of samples in the $sultp$), the spreading function f is also utilized. To prevent an adversary from fooling the system that way, the pdf of each single token t_i in h is modified by f to represent a new pdf describing the possible user location right before the creation of the next token t_{i+1}, i.e., after time $\tau(t_{i+1}) - \tau(t_i)$ since its creation. Thus a containment constraint can be modeled by a number of abidance constraints which make sure that the user stayed in the logical location not only for the complete location history, but also in the period between the last token of his last action request (given by $s(u).t_{last}$) and the first token in the new request t_0.

$$cc(l, p, e, p_e, \langle t_0, \ldots, t_n \rangle, ts) \Leftrightarrow ac(l, p, e, p_e, \langle s(u).t_{last} \rangle, \tau(t_0))$$
$$\bigwedge_{i=0}^{n-1} ac(l, p, e, p_e, \langle t_i \rangle, \tau(t_{i+1})) \wedge ac(l, p, e, p_e, \langle t_n \rangle, ts) \quad (2)$$

To constrain movement patterns to trajectories that pass a sequence of at least 2 mutually adjoining and disjunct logical locations $\boldsymbol{l} = \langle l_0, \ldots, l_m \rangle$ in their correct ordering, migration constraints mc have been defined. Since the order of traversal might be of importance, one needs to construct a partitioning $part$ of the sequence of $tokens = \langle s(u).t_{last}, t_0, \ldots, t_n \rangle$ (again starting with the last token of the previous action request), where each partition $part_i = \langle tokens_{j_i}, \ldots, tokens_{j_{i+1}-1} \rangle$ satisfies a containment constraint concerning a single logical location $l_i \in \boldsymbol{l}$.

However, one needs additionally to consider the fact that a location token could be on or near the border between both locations and thus possibly not satisfying any constraint refering to both locations. To avoid denying an action request due to such an event, the sequence $\boldsymbol{l}$ is extended with all pairwise conjunctions between adjoining locations in the path: $locs = \langle l_0, l_0 \cup l_1, l_2, \ldots, l_{m-1} \cup l_m, l_m \rangle$. Note that a partition $part_i$ can also have no elements, denoted as $part_i = \langle \rangle$ Each non-empty partition now needs to satisfy a containment constraint in $locs$ and there must at least be a non-empty partition for each $l_i \in \boldsymbol{l}$ to make sure the user was in each logical location in the right order:

$$mc(\langle l_0, \dots, l_m \rangle, p, e, p_e, \langle t_0, \dots, t_n \rangle, ts) \Leftrightarrow \exists part = \langle part_0, \dots, part_k \rangle$$

$$\bigwedge_{i=0}^{k-1} : part_i \neq \langle \rangle \Rightarrow cc(locs_i, p, e, p_e, part_i, \tau(token_{j_{i+1}}))$$

$$\wedge\, cc(locs_k, p, e, p_e, part_k, ts) \wedge \forall locs_i \in l : part_i \neq \langle \rangle \quad (3)$$

This restrictive definition of a migration constraint prevents an adversary from temporarily leaving l or stepping back to an already visited $l \in l$ and prevents shortcuts leaving out any $l \in l$.

Consistent Workflow Policies. The interaction rules in each workflow policy $\mathcal{P}(w)$ need to be defined in a way that does not exclude the processing of the workflow w in advance due to inconsistent location constraints. Furthermore, when using workflow policies, a user u may have a location history that describes a movement pattern that does not allow the transition to any succeeding action. Thus, a workflow policy $\mathcal{P}(w)$ is only called *consistent* if such situations are impossible, i.e., the following conditions are satisfied:

1. $\forall \langle a_i, a_{i+1}, lc_1 \rangle \in \mathcal{P}(w) : a_i = \bullet \rightarrow \neg (lc_1 \text{ type of } cc \vee lc_1 \text{ type of } mc)$
   (The transition from the initial action $\bullet$ to any other action a_{i+1} is not constrained with an containment or migration constraint)
2. $\forall \langle a_i, a_{i+1}, lc_1 \rangle \in \mathcal{P}(w) : a_{i+1} \neq \otimes$
   (Transitions to the abort action $\otimes$ are not constrained)
3. $\forall \langle a_i, a_{i+1}, lc_1 \rangle \in \mathcal{P}(w) : (lc_1 = cc(l, \dots) \vee lc_1 = mc(\langle l, \dots \rangle, \dots))$
   $\rightarrow \exists \langle a_{i-1}, a_i, lc_2 \rangle \in \mathcal{P}(w) : (lc_2 = cc(l, \dots) \vee lc_2 = mc(\langle \dots, l \rangle, \dots)$
   $\vee lc_2 = ac(l, \dots))$
   (If an action a_i has an outgoing transition with a containment or migration constraint in $l \in \mathcal{L}$ respectively starting in l, there needs to be at least one incoming transition with a containment or migration constraint in l respectively ending in l or at least one abidance constrained transition)
4. $\forall \langle a_i, a_{i+1}, lc_1 \rangle \in \mathcal{P}(w)\ \exists (a_i, a_{i+2}) \in \rightarrow_{\mathcal{A}} : \nexists \langle a_i, a_{i+2}, lc_2 \rangle \in \mathcal{P}(w)$
   (Each action a_i that has a constrained transition to an action a_{i+1} has at least one unconstrained transition to an action a_{i+2})

4   Example Scenario

In this section an example scenario is presented from the domain of a food production factory to demonstrate the new possibilities of the defined workflow policies. Here, hygiene and quality regulations restrict possible locations of employees to specific places and paths for certain actions. At least four logical locations are defined, having { *production hall, machine 1, laboratory, archive* } $\subseteq \mathcal{L}$. A simple workflow has been defined in the context of controlling the quality of produced food of a machine 1 in a laboratory and finally archivating this sample in an archive. This results in a workflow definition: $\mathcal{A} = \{a_1 = \textit{Take sample from}$

machine 1, a_2 =*Move to laboratory*, a_3 =*Evaluate sample*, a_4 =*Move to sample archive*, a_5 =*Archivate sample*}. And $\rightarrow_A$= { $(\bullet, a_1)$, (a_1, a_2), $(a_2, \otimes)$, (a_2, a_3), $(a_3, \otimes)$, (a_3, a_4), $(a_4, \otimes)$, (a_4, a_5), $(a_4, \otimes)$, $(a_5, \circ)$, $(a_5, \otimes)$ }. The workflow definition along with a schematic representation of the policy is depicted in Figure 4. A policy is defined that forces a user to be at *machine 1* when he starts to

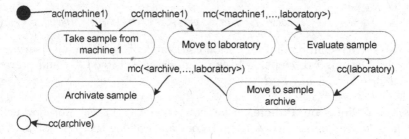

Fig. 4. A schematic representation of a workflow with an according policy from the domain of a food production factory

execute action a_1, ensuring the surveillance of the machine. In order to proceed with action a_3, he needs to migrate to the location *laboratory* in action a_2 on a predefined path that minimizes any influences on the taken sample. Again, to get a reliable result he needs to stay there for reasons of surveillance while processing the action a_3 =*Evaluate sample* in order to proceed with action a_4. Action a_4 needs to be introduced instead of a direct transition (a_3, a_5), as action a_5 forces the user to be migrated from *laboratory* to *archive* while action a_3 forces the user to be continuously in location *laboratory* which would result in an inconsistent policy if both, a migration and a containment constraint would be assigned to a possible transition (a_3, a_5).

5   Related Work

An approach to restrict the available actions of a workflow for a given user has been proposed by Atluri et al. [2]. A workflow authorization model (WAM) has been defined that restricts access to objects in accordance to the current activity of a workflow that is executed. Workflows have been extended to smart workflows where potentially mobile users interact with entities from the physical world. A methodology to abstract interfaces of those entities for smart workflows has been developed by Wieland et al. [7].

Beneath the context of mobile execution of workflows, sophisticated location based access control (LBAC) models have been developed, most of them defined as extensions to role based access control (RBAC) [8]. Here, typically RBAC-elements like roles, subjects, objects and permissions are assigned location constraints that enforce a user to be in a certain spatially bounded area. Prox-RBAC introduces two extensions on static presence or absence location predicates: Location constraints are defined using location predicates along with the keywords *when* and *while* which enforce the location predicate to be true at least at the point of time of its evaluation or until the action is completed [9]. In contrast to our approach, the set of possible subsequent actions is not reduced after a violation of a location constraint.

Special approaches for considering the uncertainty of location data in access control models have been developed: Ardagna et al. define three categories of location predicates that can be combined to expressions that need to be satisfied only at the point of time when an access request is evaluated: position constraints, interaction constraints and movement constraints [10]. An external location provider is employed to evaluate location predicates. The results are assigned a boolean value denoting the outcome of the access request along with a confidence and a timeout value obtained by the underlying location technology. If the values comply with engine-specific pre-defined thresholds, the access request is granted. Shin et al. propose an access control model that is able to define individual confidence thresholds for each access rule [4]. Only the probability of false-positives is bounded, but in contrast to our approach, nothing is said about the spatial degree or severity of errors.

Combining both, LBAC and workflow management, Decker developed an access control model for mobile workflows supporting location constraints in different levels [11]: classically constraining user-role-assignments to defined locations, constraining actions to pre-defined locations for specific roles or in general, which maps to our abidance constraints, and finally, dynamically constraining actions in a workflow to locations, where specific other actions of the workflow have been executed before. Also research on possible anomalies has been done [12]. In Decker's approach, only a relationship of the user locations between the current and the next action is evaluated. However, these approaches do not consider the movement pattern of a user during the time when an action is active.

6   Conclusion and Future Work

Transferring machine interaction from the physical domain to mobile devices brings versatile risks including unauthorized access or unforeseen and flawed results due to the lack of remote user's attendance. In this paper, an approach has been presented for partially re-coupling user locations to machine locations by defining policies which focus on user movement patterns using mobile devices that allow continuous and implicit user authentication. A WfMS called *abstract machine* has been introduced that acts as a mediator between physical machines and mobile devices based on workflow policies. For each workflow a set of rules is defined restricting for a given action the set of possible subsequent actions using location constraints. A location constraint is evaluated using a sequence of tamper-proof location measurements collected on the mobile device during the execution of a current workflow action and called a users *location history*. Three types of location constraints have been defined: abidance constraints restrict the user to be in a certain location at the point of time when he requests to proceed with the next action. Containment constraints require a user to have been within the bounds of a location without disruption during the execution period of his current action. Migration constraints require the user to have moved along a predefined path during this execution period. These constraints limit uncertainties by requiring measurements with a maximum allowed error that prove movement patterns of user's with a probability that conforms to a application specific lower bound.

Future work is seen in efficiently evaluating location constraints as delays might increase the false-negative rate of the system. Furthermore a policy specification language needs to be developed to allow to set up rules intuitively.

References

1. Bertino, E., Ferrari, E., Atluri, V.: The Specification and Enforcement of Authorization Constraints in Workflow Management Systems. ACM Transactions on Information and System Security (TISSEC) 2, 65–104 (1999)
2. Atluri, V., Huang, W.: An Authorization Model for Workflows. In: Bertino, E., Kurth, H., Martella, G., Montolivo, E. (eds.) ESORICS 1996. LNCS, vol. 1146, pp. 44–64. Springer, Heidelberg (1996)
3. Küpper, A.: Location-Based Services: Fundamentals and Operation. Wiley (2005)
4. Shin, H., Atluri, V.: Spatiotemporal Access Control Enforcement under Uncertain Location Estimates. In: Gudes, E., Vaidya, J. (eds.) Data and Applications Security 2009. LNCS, vol. 5645, pp. 159–174. Springer, Heidelberg (2009)
5. Shi, W., Yang, J., Jiang, Y., Yang, F., Xiong, Y.: SenGuard: Passive User Identification on Smartphones Using Multiple Sensors. In: 7th IEEE Int'l Conf on Wireless and Mobile Computing, Networking and Communications, pp. 141–148 (2011)
6. Gilbert, P., Cox, L., Jung, J., Wetherall, D.: Toward Trustworthy Mobile Sensing. In: Proceedings of the Eleventh Workshop on Mobile Computing Systems & Applications, HotMobile 2010, pp. 31–36. ACM (2010)
7. Wieland, M., Nicklas, D., Leymann, F.: Managing Technical Processes Using Smart Workflows. In: Mähönen, P., Pohl, K., Priol, T. (eds.) ServiceWave 2008. LNCS, vol. 5377, pp. 287–298. Springer, Heidelberg (2008)
8. van Cleeff, A., Pieters, W., Wieringa, R.: Benefits of Location-Based Access Control: A Literature Study. In: Proceedings of the 2010 IEEE/ACM Int'l Conf on Green Computing and Communications & Int'l Conf on Cyber, Physical and Social Computing, GREENCOM-CPSCOM 2010, pp. 739–746. IEEE (2010)
9. Kirkpatrick, M., Damiani, M., Bertino, E.: Prox-RBAC: A Proximity-based Spatially Aware RBAC. In: Proceedings of the 19th ACM SIGSPATIAL Int'l Conf on Advances in Geographic Information Systems, GIS 2011, pp. 339–348. ACM (2011)
10. Ardagna, C., Cremonini, M., Damiani, E., di Vimercati, S., Samarati, P.: Supporting Location-Based Conditions in Access Control Policies. In: Proceedings of the 2006 ACM Symposium on Information, Computer and Communications Security, ASIACCS 2006, pp. 212–222. ACM (2006)
11. Decker, M., Stürzel, P., Klink, S., Oberweis, A.: Location Constraints for Mobile Workflows. In: Proceedings of the 2009 Conf. on Techniques and Applications for Mobile Commerce, TAMoCo 2009, pp. 93–102. IOS Press (2009)
12. Che, H., Decker, M.: Anomalies in Business Process Models for Mobile Scenarios with Location Constraints. In: Proceedings of the IEEE Int'l Conf on Automation and Logistics, ICAL 2010, pp. 306–313. IEEE (2010)

PEPPeR: A Querier's Privacy Enhancing Protocol for PaRticipatory Sensing

Tassos Dimitriou[1], Ioannis Krontiris[2], and Ahmad Sabouri[2]

[1] Athens Information Technology, 19.5 km Markopoulo Ave., 19002, Peania, Greece
tdim@ait.edu.gr
[2] Goethe University Frankfurt, Chair of Mobile Business & Multilateral Security,
Grueneburgplatz 1, 60323 Frankfurt, Germany
{ioannis.krontiris,ahmad.sabouri}@m-chair.net

Abstract. In this work we study the problem of querier privacy in the Participatory Sensing domain. While prior work has attempted to protect the privacy of people contributing sensing data from their mobile phones, little or no work has focused on the problem of *querier privacy*. Motivated by a novel communication model in which clients may directly query participatory sensing networks operated by potentially untrusted adversaries, we propose PEPPeR, a protocol for privacy-preserving access control in participatory sensing applications that focuses on the privacy of the querier. Contrary to past solutions, PEPPeR enables queriers to have access to the data provided by participating users without placing any trust in third parties or reducing the scope of queries. Additionally, our approach naturally extends the traditional pull/push models of participatory sensing and integrates nicely with mobile social networks, a new breed of sensing which combines mobile sensor devices with personal sensing environments.

1 Introduction

The increasing availability of sensors on today's smartphones and other everyday devices, carried around by millions of people, has already opened up new possibilities for gathering sensed information from our environment. Currently researchers experiment with these possibilities and share the vision of a sensor data-sharing infrastructure, where people and their mobile devices provide their collected data streams in accessible ways to third parties interested in integrating and remixing the data for a specific purpose. A popular example is a noise mapping application which generates collective noise maps by aggregating measurements provided by the mobile phones of volunteers [1]. In other scenarios, people may monitor air pollution [2], road and traffic conditions [3], etc.

What is common in all the above applications, is that sensing data are proactively collected by users in a centralized server, where they are aggregated, processed and represented through various interfaces (e.g. statistical data on a map) or remain available for third parties to query and select data of interest. While this serves a specific class of applications, another approach is to enable the collection of sensing information only where and when it is needed. In that sense,

A.U. Schmidt et al. (Eds.): MOBISEC 2012, LNICST 107, pp. 93–106, 2012.
© Institute for Computer Sciences, Social Informatics and Telecommunications Engineering 2012

someone interested to obtain information from a specific location and within a specific context, posts a task or query to the platform and the mobile nodes satisfying the conditions react by taking the measurements and sending back a response.

In this paradigm, the question becomes how these sensing tasks can be distributed to the mobile phones. Two models have been studied in the bibliography so far. In the *push* model [4], the participating nodes (i.e. mobile phones) register with the server and the server pushes only matching tasks, based on appropriate context (e.g. location). In the *pull* model [5], sensing tasks are posted on a server, which participating nodes contact for possible download and execution of tasks.

In this work, we consider an extension to the participatory sensing model, in which a user may decide to query a participating node *directly*, without the mediation of the service provider. Contrary to the traditional model, where reporting of data is performed through a trusted report server (e.g. Anonysense), this method maybe the only feasible solution when it is impossible or even undesirable to maintain a stable connection between a mobile user and the service provider. It is also necessitated by the growing requirement for protecting users' data access privacy; a user may want to keep confidential whether (and when) she accessed the sensed data, the data types she was interested in, or from which nodes she obtained the data, as the disclosure of such information may be used against her interest. For example, information about the noise level in a particular neighborhood may leak information to the nearby home agency about Alice's desire to purchase a home in the area.

Additionally, the sensed data maybe of interest to numerous users from both the public and private sectors, ranging from individuals to business companies that may be competing of each other. To capitalize on the data, application owners might be using appropriate incentive mechanisms [6] to enable broad user participation. It is reasonable, therefore, to expect that queriers are willing to pay appropriate fees in order to obtain measurements of interest.

Our method seems also to be a perfect fit for a new breed of sensing, triggered by the ever increasing number of online Social Network users and the imminent integration of mobile sensor devices into personal sensing environments [7,8]. Such *mobile social networks* are distributed systems that combine mobile, social, and sensing components, trying to create a contextual picture surrounding a user or group of users in order to enable new applications and services based on this context. In this new model of P2P sensing, it is thus straightforward to expect that users may ask other peers directly for sensed data. In fact this may be the only way to hide a querier's interest on certain data since, with any centralized service, a user's interests and queries may leak information about the user itself. Thus the goal of this work is to describe a generic mechanism in which queriers may ask directly for sensed data.

Contribution: In this work, we present PEPPeR (Privacy Enhancing Protocol for PaRticipatory sensing), that aims to protect the privacy of queriers, by letting them obtain *tokens* from the service provider (or application owner) in order to have access to the data provided by participating users (custodians of mobile phones). The difference from prior work is in the decentralized character of our approach. The querier may decide to spend the token with *any* producer (mobile phone user) directly, who first has to validate the token and then provide the querier with the proper amount of requested data. Using appropriate cryptographic mechanisms, we show how the validity of the token can be verified by any mobile node, without, however, leaking the identity of the querier to the node or to the application owner. At the heart of PEPPeR lies a mechanism to detect double-spent tokens, which involves the use of a witnesses service, a simple scheme that can attest to the validity of the token or provide proof for token reuse.

2   Related Work

Privacy preserving access control has been studied extensively in traditional sensor networks ([9,10,11,12]). While the work in [9] is a centralized approach in which users acquire data through one or more base stations, the rest take advantage of the inherent redundancy in sensor networks to either store and discover double-spent tokens ([10]) or forward queries in a privacy-preserving manner ([11,12]). However, all proposed solutions are based on the multi-hop routing communication model of sensor networks in which nodes operate both as sensing devices and routers of information, a model that cannot be adopted in participatory sensing.

In the participatory sensing domain, various *centralized* solutions for distributing tasks or queries to sensor nodes have been proposed. In PRISM [4], participating nodes (i.e. mobile phones) register with the server and the server tracks the nodes and pushes only matching tasks to them, based on their context (e.g. location). For example, Alice may be assigned the task "measure temperature in area X", when she is entering this area. However, this solution does not consider privacy for any of the involved entities, queriers or mobile nodes.

A solution that offers a privacy-friendly way of task distribution is Anony-Sense [5]. Sensing tasks are posted on a server and the participating nodes download the tasks and match them to their context to decide which one to execute. This approach has the advantage that the nodes do not reveal anything about their context to the service provider, in order to receive the sensing task. Still, AnonySense does not consider privacy for the entities posting the tasks.

Recently, PEPSI [13] was suggested as a system designed with the privacy of the queriers in mind, queriers being entities external to the platform, who are interested in some specific sensing information. PEPSI is based on a *centralized* solution and to protect the privacy of the queriers, it introduces a Registration Authority, a trusted third party which collects queries from the queriers and provides back the corresponding cryptographic material. In that sense, the queries reach the platform in an encrypted form. However, the problem is shifted to the Registration Authority, where essentially all queries are known in advance, along with the identities of the queriers, leading to the assumption that this entity must be trusted.

PEPSI is designed to work in a different setting than the one suggested in this paper. Due to the cryptographic mechanism employed by the protocol, queries have to be composed out of specific, *predefined* keywords. At the same time, mobile nodes *proactively* sense and report data, including the same keywords. At the end, following a centralized communication paradigm, queries and sensing data are both collected by the service provider, where they are matched against each other.

3   Network Model and Security Goals

The main goal of PEPPeR is to protect the privacy of the parties posting sensing queries or tasks to mobile nodes. To do this efficiently, we *decouple* the process of discovering the nodes that are able to answer a query from the access control mechanisms utilized in the system to contact these nodes. This is due to the fact that each of these processes concerns a different entity in the system. From a platform provider's point of view, no matter how a querier finds her desired mobile nodes, it is critical to stop her from making benefit of the platform's services without getting permission from the provider. How this permission can be obtained depends on the business model of the platform provider. For example, it could be that the querier has to pay for each "sensing quantum". On the other hand, from the querier's perspective, no matter what access control mechanism is employed in the system, she should be able to communicate with any mobile node in a privacy-respecting way, without disclosing her interest to the provider.

Figure 1 depicts this setting and shows the focus of PEPPeR. The role of the service provider is limited only to providing the means for queriers to contact the mobile nodes. That is, mobile nodes first register with the platform and through a privacy-respecting mechanism (agnostic to this paper) the service provider is able to offer the querier the contact details (e.g. in anonymous or pseudonymous way) of the mobile nodes currently in the geographic area of interest. For example, this could be achieved through a distributed directory service for looking up mobile nodes.

In addition, the querier anonymously purchases a cryptographic token from the platform, which enables her to directly contact the mobile nodes and forward the query to them. Due to the cryptographic properties of this token, there is no need to restrict the scope of the queries or introduce a trusted third party, as in past works.

The privacy of the mobile nodes still needs to be protected and our work at no means hinders protocols built for this purpose. However this work is *not* about how to a) support the discovery of sensor information, b) allow for sensor subscription, and c) facilitate sensor task placement. These topics have been covered, to some extend, by prior work [4,5,7] and are not considered here. Here we address the topic of querier privacy that can be of value to the various denominations of participatory sensing networks.

Given the above setting, the following security and privacy goals are required to be fulfilled by the access control mechanism:

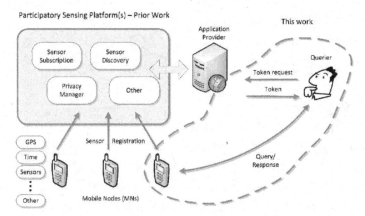

Fig. 1. Query privacy in the context of participatory sensing

- *Untraceability*: In order to preserve the querier's privacy, the access control mechanism should not leak any information about the identity of the authorized querier, when she contacts the service provider.
- *Unlinkability*: A single querier can use the platform as many times as she is allowed to, in order to access and query mobile nodes. It should not be possible to link multiple accesses back to the same quierier, as long as she is eligible and has the access credentials to use the service.
- *Misuse Resistance*: The access control mechanism should prohibit unauthorized users from using the system. In addition, it should also prevent queriers from misusing the service, according to the conditions agreed upon. For example, if the querier acquired credentials for accessing and querying the nodes only one-time, then she should not be able to reuse them for a second time.
- *Misuse Provability*: The access control mechanism should support providing evidence, in case of a misuse. For example, if the querier is permitted to use the platform only once and makes a second attempt, the access control mechanism should be able to provide convincing proof of the fact that this is the second time access. This will enable mobile nodes to deny service, however the privacy of the querier should still be respected.

4   Querier Privacy Protocol

In this section, we present the protocol behind PEPPeR that satisfies the above requirements and offers a privacy-respecting access control for querying mobile nodes of interest. Figure 2 shows a high-level overview of the steps, which we will describe in detail in the following sections.

A querier $\mathcal{Q}$ wishes to access the participatory sensing network for data. She first contacts the application owner $\mathcal{S}$ and retrieves a token $\mathcal{T}$ which can spent with any producer $\mathcal{P}$ (mobile phone user) of sensed data (Section 4.1). The token reveals no information about either $\mathcal{Q}$ or the desire of $\mathcal{Q}$ to spend it with any

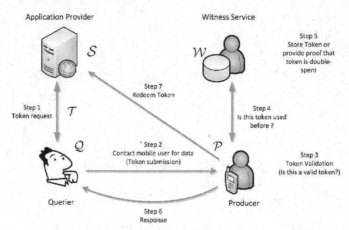

Fig. 2. The protocol steps followed by PEPPeR

specific $\mathcal{P}$. Once $\mathcal{P}$ retrieves the token, it first has to verify its validity and then test whether the token is an attempt of doublespending (Section 4.2). For that reason it contacts an appropriate witness service $\mathcal{W}$ which can either ascertain the coin's freshness or provide proof that the coin has been doublespent (Section 4.2). This service can have the form of a bulletin board (a simple repository of used tokens) in which nodes may consult for reused tokens. The evidence provided by $\mathcal{W}$ again reveals nothing about the identity of the querier $\mathcal{Q}$, only the fact that the coin has been used before. Finally, the producer $\mathcal{P}$ can redeem the token for credit or additional services from $\mathcal{S}$. These steps are shown in Figure 2 and are described in more detail below.

4.1   Purchasing a Token

To make a request for sensor data, a querier $\mathcal{Q}$ must first obtain a valid token from the application provider. In order to make the token untraceable and protect the privacy of $\mathcal{Q}$, the token will not be associated with a particular querier, however it should contain such information as date, expiration date and amount of data to be retrieved as well as the signature of the application provider $\mathcal{S}$ on it. This information is the *common part* of the token which is necessary in order for the mobile user (supplier of sensed data) to be able to provide a commensurate amount of information and perform an initial test on the validity of the token (i.e. check expiration date and signature of $\mathcal{S}$).

As the token can be purchased by $\mathcal{Q}$ through an anonymous channel using (say) a gift card or a trusted third party, the common part of the coin, denoted by $\langle CommonInfo \rangle$, leaks no information about the identity of $\mathcal{Q}$. We need, however, to provide a mechanism for detecting double spending, and this mechanism has to be associated with *identifying* information, denoted by $\langle UniqueInfo \rangle$, supplied by the querier $\mathcal{Q}$. This uniquely identifying piece of information is in no way related to the identity of $\mathcal{Q}$; its purpose is to deter double spending but it could potentially be used by $\mathcal{S}$ to trace the token and this is why it has to be *blinded* before it is signed by $\mathcal{S}$.

Blind signatures provide perfect confidentiality to a message and signature pair, however the signer must be assured that the message contains valid information in order to prevent abuse [14]. This valid information corresponds to the $\langle CommonInfo \rangle$ part. An elegant solution to cope with the necessity of checking the correctness of messages contained in blind signatures is to use the so-called *partially* blind signatures introduced in [15]. In our scenario, the provider $\mathcal{S}$ will sign messages made of two parts; the $\langle CommonInfo \rangle$ part which is visible by the signer and the $\langle UniqueInfo \rangle$ part containing identifying information to detect double spending which is invisible and blindly signed. An instantiation of this process is described below.

Let k be the security parameter. Let p' and q' be two large primes of size $k/2$ such that $p = 2p' + 1$ and $q = 2q' + 1$ are also prime. Let $N = pq$ be an RSA modulus, (e, N) be the public key of the application provider $\mathcal{S}$ and (d, N) its corresponding private key in the RSA key generation process. Following the general method outlined in [15], one way to include common information to any message m is to *embed* it in the signer's key and generate new, per message signing keys (in our case per token keys). So, let $h()$ be a secure cryptographic hash function such as SHA1. The new public (and private) exponent e_T (resp. d_T) for token $\mathcal{T}$, generated from e, is obtained as follows:

Algorithm 1
Creating partial signature keys from (e, N)

$$h_1 \leftarrow h(e, \langle CommonInfo \rangle)$$
$$e_T \leftarrow h_1 \parallel h(h_1) \parallel 00000001$$
$$d_T \leftarrow 1/e_T \mod \phi(N)$$

The existence of the inverse, signing keys d_T is due to the following facts. Since $N = (2p'+1)(2q'+1)$, we have $\phi(N) = 4p'q'$. Both p' and q' are large primes (ca. 511 bits) while the concatenation $h_1 \parallel h(h_1)$ is 320 bits long. In addition, e_T is enforced to be an odd integer, hence it is not divisible by any of $\{2, 4, p', q'\}$. Thus e_T is relatively prime to $\phi(N)$ and has an inverse d_T, which can be computed by $\mathcal{S}$. Additionally, a secure RSA setting requires the decryption key to be larger than $\sqrt{N}$ [16]. This is guaranteed by making e_T around 320 bits long which ensures that d_T will be longer than 512 bits in case of 1024-bit modulus. (*The proof of resistance to chosen message attacks of signatures generated this way is shown in the Appendix.*)

A querier $\mathcal{Q}$ can ask the service provider to provide a token by using the procedure shown in Protocol 1. Recall that $\langle UniqueInfo \rangle$ is the part that has to be blinded and contains identifying information to prevent double spending (the exact format of this part will become clear in the next section). Let also r be a random number in Z_N and $m = h(\langle UniqueInfo \rangle)$.

Protocol 1
Obtaining a blind signature from $\mathcal{S}$

1. $\mathcal{Q}$ sends $m^* = m r^{e_T} \bmod N$ to $\mathcal{S}$ by evaluating the public key e_T from public information available (e.g. e and $\langle CommonInfo \rangle$).
2. The application owner $\mathcal{S}$ returns the signature $\sigma^* = (m^*)^{d_T} \bmod N$ to $\mathcal{Q}$.
3. $\mathcal{Q}$ computes $\sigma = r^{-1}\sigma^* \bmod N$, which is the application owner's signature on $h(\langle UniqueInfo \rangle)$.

Due to the blinding factor r, the network owner cannot derive m and σ from m^*. In other words, given $\langle m, \sigma \rangle$, the network owner cannot link it to $\mathcal{Q}$. Additionally, since the $\langle CommonInfo \rangle$ part is clear to the querier and is negotiated at the beginning of (or before) the protocol, $\mathcal{S}$ cannot include any information in it and hence trace the querier. An implicit assumption here is that the parameters in the common part do not contain any one-time elements that may help distinguish the transaction and narrow down the search such as for example a strange combination of date and amount of data, and so on. If this is a concern, users may depend on a trusted third party to purchase tokens or use alternative schemes such as anonymous gift cards. Once the signature σ is retrieved, the final token becomes $\mathcal{T} = \langle CommonInfo, UniqueInfo, m, \sigma \rangle$.

4.2   Spending and Redeeming a Token

Let $\mathcal{P}$ be the producer of data (mobile phone user) that $\mathcal{Q}$ has decided to spend the token to. In order to provide the required amount of sensed data, $\mathcal{Q}$ has to be able to tell if the token $\mathcal{T}$ has been used before. For that reason, $\mathcal{P}$ will contact the *witness* service $\mathcal{W}$ in order to attest on the validity of $\mathcal{T}$ or provide proof that the token has been used before. Crucial to the above is the structure of the $\langle UniqueInfo \rangle$ existing in $\mathcal{T}$. This element will allow $\mathcal{P}$ (as well as $\mathcal{W}$) to provide the necessary evidence for the token's validity.

Let P and Q be primes such that $Q | P - 1$ and g a generator of order Q in the group Z_P^*. Typically, P and Q will have length 1024 bits and 160 bits, respectively. The querier $\mathcal{Q}$ will select two secret values $s, r \in Z_P$ and compute $v = g^{-s} \bmod P$ and $x = g^r \bmod P$. The $\langle UniqueInfo \rangle$ element will consist of the two values v and x, which will be signed by $\mathcal{S}$ as explained in the previous section.

When the querier wishes to spend the token $\mathcal{T}$, it will first have to demonstrate the *validity* of the coin by proving knowledge of the two secret values s, r using appropriate zero-knowledge proofs. This protocol is based on the identification scheme of Schnorr [17] (see also Okamoto [18] for a generalization and [19] for an instantiation on the e-cash setting) and can be made non-interactive by making the challenge of the verifier equal to the hash value of the token and committed protocol parameters. The interaction between $\mathcal{Q}$ and $\mathcal{P}$ is shown below.

Protocol 2

Checking the validity of a token $\mathcal{T}$

1. $\mathcal{Q}$ sends $\mathcal{P}$ $\langle \mathcal{T}, y, date/time \rangle$, where $y = r + es \mod Q$ and $e = h(\langle \mathcal{T}, date/time \rangle)$.
2. $\mathcal{P}$ verifies the signature of $\mathcal{S}$ on the token and checks that $x = g^y v^e \mod P$.

If the tests in Step 2 of Protocol 2 succeed, $\mathcal{P}$ considers the token *valid*. However, $\mathcal{P}$ still has to determine whether the token is *fresh* or an attempt of doublespending. For that reason it has to contact the witness service $\mathcal{W}$ that can attest on the freshness of the token. The interaction between $\mathcal{P}$ and a $\mathcal{W}$ is shown below:

Protocol 3

Checking for doublespending

1. $\mathcal{P}$ sends $\mathcal{W}$ the transcript of the interaction with $\mathcal{Q}$, i.e. $\langle \mathcal{T}, y, date/time \rangle$.
2. $\mathcal{W}$ verifies the signature of $\mathcal{S}$ on $\mathcal{T}$ and checks that $x = g^y v^e \mod P$. Then, based on the expiration date of the token, searches its records for a token containing the same $\langle UniqueInfo \rangle$ element. If no match is found, the token is considered fresh and $\mathcal{W}$ records the values $\langle \mathcal{T}, y, date/time \rangle$.

   If a match is found then $\mathcal{W}$ returns evidence that the token has been used before. This evidence has the form of the secret values s, r selected by $\mathcal{Q}$ in forming the values v and x contained in the $\langle UniqueInfo \rangle$ element.

To see why $\mathcal{W}$ can provide evidence[1] that a token has been used before, notice that in this case it will have two transcripts $\langle \mathcal{T}, y, date/time \rangle$ and $\langle \mathcal{T}, y', date'/time' \rangle$ such that $x = g^y v^e \mod P$ and $x = g^{y'} v^{e'} \mod P$. $\mathcal{W}$ can then compute $s = (y - y')/(e - e') \mod Q$ by solving

$$y = r + es \mod Q,$$
$$y' = r + e's \mod Q.$$

In a similar manner $\mathcal{W}$ can obtain r. Notice that these values are not connected with the ID of $\mathcal{Q}$, hence they are not used in identifying $\mathcal{Q}$. They are only used to provide evidence that a token has been double-spent. Hence the privacy of $\mathcal{Q}$ is maintained even in this case.

Once $\mathcal{P}$ is convinced that the token is both valid and fresh, it can provide the data requested by $\mathcal{Q}$. Then it can go on redeeming the token in exchange for other

---

[1] Alternatively, $\mathcal{W}$ returns the previous transcript $\langle \mathcal{T}, y', date'/time' \rangle$ and $\mathcal{P}$ can check itself if the coin is not used before.

services or credit provided by the application provider. A slight complication might arise, however, if $\mathcal{P}$ redeems the token but *denies* to offer $\mathcal{Q}$ the data she "paid" for. A solution to this problem is for $\mathcal{Q}$ to ask for a signed commitment from $\mathcal{P}$ that it will provide the data, assuming the token is both valid and fresh. This exchange can have the form shown below and should be executed before Step 1 of Protocol 2.

$$\mathcal{Q} \rightarrow \mathcal{P} : h(\mathcal{T}), N_Q$$
$$\mathcal{P} \rightarrow \mathcal{Q} : Sig_{\mathcal{P}}(h(\mathcal{T}), N_Q, \text{"Commit to Serve"})$$

The signature on the second message is a commitment that $\mathcal{P}$ agrees to serve the token that hashes to $h(\mathcal{T})$. Once $\mathcal{Q}$ verifies the signature, it proceeds with the remaining steps of Protocol 2.

5   Security Analysis

In this section, we demonstrate the security properties of the protocol which match the goals set forth in Section 3. Some are new (Appendix) and some are inherited by the use of appropriate cryptographic protocols used throughout.

Token Unforgeability: The process described in Section 4.1 (Algorithm 1) of embedding common information in the signer's key has been proven secure in the Appendix. This is another contribution of this paper since in the work of [15], no concrete method has been presented. Thus, a token obtained during token purchase cannot be altered by a querier without affecting the validity of the signature. In a similar manner, no querier can create a valid token without knowledge of the secret signing keys. Security is based on the hash-then-sign paradigm of RSA and the strength of hash functions acting as random oracles.

Token Untraceability: Due to blindness, the only information learnt by $\mathcal{S}$ is the $\langle CommonInfo \rangle$ element. Going back to Protocol 1, $\mathcal{S}$ cannot derive $h(\langle UniqueInfo \rangle)$ and σ from m^*, without knowing the blinding factor r. In other words, given the pair $(h(\langle UniqueInfo \rangle), \sigma)$, the application owner cannot link it to a querier $\mathcal{Q}$. Thus when a token is redeemed by a producer $\mathcal{P}$, the application owner will not be able to tell which querier requested the token.

An implicit assumption here is that the $\langle CommonInfo \rangle$ element used to create the signing key in Algorithm 1 does not contain any information that can be used to identify this particular transaction. If this is the case, $\mathcal{Q}$ may simply deny to take part in the token generation process.

However, even if it's difficult to associate tokens with the identities of their holders, the application owner may still narrow down the owner of a particular token to the queriers who purchased tokens. This might be a concern if the number of token buyers is limited. In such a case, users may rely on trusted third parties to purchase tokens from $\mathcal{S}$.

Double Spending Prevention: Resilience to double spending is due to the construction of the $\langle UniqueInfo \rangle$ element. This element consists of the two values v and x which are equal to $v = g^{-s} \mod P$ and $x = g^r \mod P$, respectively. When a querier $\mathcal{Q}$ sends the value y to $\mathcal{P}$ (recall Protocol 2) essentially proves knowledge of the values r and s that make up v and x.

One strategy, therefore, that $\mathcal{Q}$ can use to double spend a token $\mathcal{T}$ is to come up with a different representation of the values v and x. But that's equivalent to computing discrete logarithms [19], which is considered an intractable problem. In a similar manner, no other querier will be able to double spent this token as it would have to prove the token's validity (Protocol 2) first. But that would also require knowledge of the values r and s, otherwise the NIZK protocol would fail. Thus, we conclude that a token cannot be used more than once.

Finally, it is clear from Protocol 3 that if $\mathcal{Q}$ tries to double spend a token $\mathcal{T}$, then a producer can recover the secret values making up v and x, thus providing evidence that a coin has been double-spent.

Querier's Privacy: PEPPeR preserves the querier's privacy and fulfils all the requirements of Section 3. There are several potential points where the querier's privacy can get compromised. We briefly discuss below, how our solution copes with these cases.

Token Purchase. Whenever a financial transaction is involved in the scenario, there is a risk of linkability to the real identity of the buyer (in our case the querier) if the underlying payment methods are not privacy preserving. PEPPeR is independent from the credit transfer mechanism, so if it is done in a privacy friendly way, the whole operation will not leak any identifying information about the querier.

Mobile Node Lookup. The access control mechanism is designed to abstract away the mobile node lookup process. As a result, the level of privacy achieved by the query delivery method in the platform will stay unaffected by PEPPeR. For example, a distributed directory service by the mobile nodes can elevate the privacy level significantly, compared to the existing query-task matching schemes by a centralized server that can be found frequently in the literature (e.g. [13]). Integrating PEPPeR to any such a privacy-friendly method will not have any negative impact and will not introduce any new risk to existing systems.

Token Spending. When a querier wants to retrieve data from a Mobile Node and spend her access token, she cannot be identified or linked to the purchase phase. The cryptography used underneath enables us to break the connection between these two steps and prevent any correlation between purchase and spending phase. Therefore, even if the identity of the querier was somehow revealed while purchasing the token, she can ensure that the usage of the token will stay unlinkable to her. The other important aspect of PEPPeR is that misuse and double-spending cases can be detected and proved without a need for disclosing querier's identity information.

6 Conclusions and Future Work

In this paper, we have considered the problem of query privacy in people-centric sensing networks, in which queriers do not need to trust and rely on a service provider (or application owner) S, in order to get access to the data produced by mobile users. We have described PEPPeR, a generic protocol that protects querier's privacy, by letting a querier Q obtain tokens from S, which reveal nothing about either the identity of Q or its desire to spend the token with a *specific* supplier of sensed data. Using appropriate cryptographic mechanisms to ensure token validity, double-spending prevention, etc., PEPPeR does not restrict the scope of queries or introduce trusted third parties as in past solutions; the role of the service provider is limited only to providing the means for queriers to contact the mobile nodes, a service which can be agnostic to our protocol.

As part of a future work, we are planning to integrate our protocol with traditional sensing platforms, even social ones, in order to further demonstrate the applicability and viability of our approach. An interesting point of research would also be to eliminate entirely the witness service provided centrally for double-spent tokens and replace it with one by which mobile users *themselves* would be able to attest the validity of tokens. While such methods have been considered in traditional P2P systems (see for example the work in [20] in the e-cash setting and the references therein), these methods generally assume the presence of witnesses *at all times*. This would be difficult to assume in the case of participatory/social sensing, in which nodes are free to come and go as they like. Additionally, these nodes may become single points of failure or introduce collusion in the token spending process. Hence more robust mechanisms are needed to ensure the validity of such a (distributed) witness service in terms of persistence, consistency as well as scalability.

Acknowledgements. The first author would like to thank Angelos Kiayias for useful discussions. This work has been funded by the European Community's FP7 project SafeCity (Grant Agreement no: 285556).

References

1. Maisonneuve, N., Stevens, M., Ochab, B.: Participatory noise pollution monitoring using mobile phones. Information Policy 15, 51–71 (2010)
2. Honicky, R., Brewer, E.A., Paulos, E., White, R.: N-smarts: networked suite of mobile atmospheric real-time sensors. In: Proceedings of the 2nd ACM SIGCOMM workshop on Networked systems for developing regions (NSDR 2008), pp. 25–30 (2008)
3. Mohan, P., Padmanabhan, V.N., Ramjee, R.: Nericell: rich monitoring of road and traffic conditions using mobile smartphones. In: Proceedings of the 6th ACM Conference on Embedded Network Sensor Systems (SenSys 2008), pp. 323–336 (2008)

4. Das, T., Mohan, P., Padmanabhan, V.N., Ramjee, R., Sharma, A.: PRISM: platform for remote sensing using smartphones. In: Proceedings of the 8th International Conference on Mobile Systems, Applications, and Services (MobiSys 2010), San Francisco, California, USA, pp. 63–76 (2010)

5. Shin, M., Cornelius, C., Peebles, D., Kapadia, A., Kotz, D., Triandopoulos, N.: AnonySense: A system for anonymous opportunistic sensing. Journal of Pervasive and Mobile Computing (2010)

6. Krontiris, I., Albers, A.: Monetary incentives in participatory sensing using multi-attributive auctions. International Journal of Parallel, Emergent and Distributed Systems (2012)

7. Beach, A., Gartrell, M., Xing, X., Han, R., Lv, Q., Mishra, S., Seada, K.: Fusing mobile, sensor, and social data to fully enable context-aware computing. In: Proceedings of the 11th Workshop on Mobile Computing Systems & Applications (HotMobile 2010), Annapolis, Maryland, pp. 60–65 (2010)

8. Krontiris, I., Freiling, F.C.: Integrating people-centric sensing with social networks: A privacy research agenda. In: Proceeding of the IEEE International Workshop on Security and Social Networking, SESOC (2010)

9. Carbunar, B., Yu, Y., Shi, W., Pearce, M., Vasudevan, V.: Query privacy in wireless sensor networks. ACM Transactions on Sensor Networks 6(2) (2010)

10. Zhang, R., Zhang, Y., Ren, K.: DP2AC: Distributed Privacy-Preserving Access Control in Sensor Networks. In: Proceeding of the 28th Conference on Computer Communications, INFOCOM 2009 (2009)

11. De Cristofaro, E., Ding, X., Tsudik, G.: Privacy-preserving querying in sensor networks. In: Proceeding of the International Conference on Computer Communications and Networks, ICCCN 2009 (2009)

12. Dimitriou, T., Sabouri, A.: Privacy preservation schemes for querying wireless sensor networks. In: Proceedings of the 7th IEEE PerCom International Workshop on Sensor Networks and Systems for Pervasive Computing (PerSeNS 2011), pp. 178–183 (2011)

13. De Cristofaro, E., Soriente, C.: Short paper: PEPSI – privacy-enhanced participatory sensing infrastructure. In: Proceedings of the Fourth ACM Conference on Wireless Network Security (WiSec 2011), pp. 23–28 (2011)

14. Chaum, D.: Blind signatures for untraceable payments. In: CRYPTO, pp. 199–203 (1982)

15. Abe, M., Fujisaki, E.: How to Date Blind Signatures. In: Kim, K.-C., Matsumoto, T. (eds.) ASIACRYPT 1996. LNCS, vol. 1163, pp. 244–251. Springer, Heidelberg (1996)

16. Boneh, D.: Twenty Years of Attacks on the RSA Cryptosystem. Notices of the American Mathematical Society (AMS) 46(2), 203–213 (1999)

17. Schnorr, C.P.: Efficient signature generation by smart cards. Journal of Cryptology 4(3), 161–174 (1991)

18. Okamoto, T.: Provably Secure and Practical Identification Schemes and Corresponding Signature Schemes. In: Brickell, E.F. (ed.) CRYPTO 1992. LNCS, vol. 740, pp. 31–53. Springer, Heidelberg (1993)

19. Brands, S.: Untraceable Off-Line Cash in Wallets with Observers (Extended Abstract). In: Stinson, D.R. (ed.) CRYPTO 1993. LNCS, vol. 773, pp. 302–318. Springer, Heidelberg (1994)

20. Osipkov, I., Vasserman, E.Y., Hopper, N., Kim, Y.: Combating double-spending using cooperative P2P systems. In: Proceedings of the 27th International Conference on Distributed Computing Systems, ICDCS 2007 (2007)

21. Bellare, M., Rogaway, P.: The Exact Security of Digital Signatures - How to Sign with RSA and Rabin. In: Maurer, U.M. (ed.) EUROCRYPT 1996. LNCS, vol. 1070, pp. 399–416. Springer, Heidelberg (1996)
22. Coron, J.-S.: On the Exact Security of Full Domain Hash. In: Bellare, M. (ed.) CRYPTO 2000. LNCS, vol. 1880, pp. 229–235. Springer, Heidelberg (2000)

Appendix

In this section we prove the security of signatures against chosen message attacks when multiple signing keys are generated from the same public/private key pair (Algorithm 1). The reader is referred to [21,22] for the various definitions.

More precisely, we define an extension to the Full Domain Hash Signature scheme in which the key generation algorithm on input 1^k generates various public/private key pairs (N, e_i, d_i), as in Algorithm 1, and the signing/verification algorithms have oracle access to a hash function $H_{FDH} : \{0,1\}^* \to Z_N^*$. We will now relate the security of this scheme to the security of solving the RSA problem (i.e. recovering a plaintext from an encrypted message).

Proof (high level) Let $\mathcal{F}$ be a forger that breaks the extended FDH. Using $\mathcal{F}$, we will build an inverter $\mathcal{I}$ that can be used to break RSA. The goal of $\mathcal{I}$ is to find $x = f^{-1}(y)$ for some key e_i and a random $y \in Z_N^*$, where f is the RSA exponentiation function.

The inverter starts by running $\mathcal{F}$. When $\mathcal{F}$ makes hash and signing queries, $\mathcal{I}$ answer those itself. In particular, when $\mathcal{F}$ makes a hash oracle query for M, the inverter increments a counter i, sets $M_i = M$ and picks a random $r_i \in Z_N^*$. It then returns $h_i = r_i^{e_1 e_2 \cdots e_k} \mod N$ with probability p and $h_i = y r_i^{e_1 e_2 \cdots e_k} \mod N$ with probability $1-p$. It also maintains all $r_i^{e_1 e_2 \cdots e_k / e_j}$ values, $1 \le j \le k$, for simulating the signing oracle.

Eventually, $\mathcal{F}$ halts and outputs a forgery (M, s) for some public key e_i (wlog. assume this is e_1). We also assume that $\mathcal{F}$ has requested the hash of M before. If not, $\mathcal{I}$ goes ahead and makes the hash query itself, so that in any case $M = M_i$ for some i.

Then, if $h_i = y r_i^{e_1 e_2 \cdots e_k} \mod N$ we have $s = h^{d_1} = y^{d_1} r_i^{e_2 \cdots e_k} \mod N$ and $\mathcal{I}$ outputs $y^{d_1} (= s / r_i^{e_2 \cdots e_k} \mod N)$ as the inverse for y. Thus the intractability of the RSA problem is reduced to the intractability of the extended FDH signing algorithm. Also by tuning the probability p, we can make the probability of forging a signature almost equally low as inverting RSA (details omitted due to space restrictions, refer to [21,22] for similar arguments). This proves the correctness of the signature generation process.

Using Extracted Behavioral Features to Improve Privacy for Shared Route Tracks

Mads Schaarup Andersen, Mikkel Baun Kjærgaard, and Kaj Grønbæk

Department of Computer Science,
Aarhus University
{masa,mikkelbk,kgronbak}@cs.au.dk

Abstract. Track-based services, such as road pricing, usage-based insurance, and sports trackers, require users to share entire tracks of locations, however this may seriously violate users' privacy. Existing privacy methods suffer from the fact that they degrade service quality when adding privacy. In this paper, we present the concept of *privacy by substitution* that addresses the problem without degrading service quality by substituting location tracks with less privacy invasive behavioral data extracted from raw tracks of location data or other sensing data. We explore this concept by designing and implementing *TracM*, a track-based community service for runners to share and compare their running performance. We show how such a service can be implemented by substituting location tracks with less privacy invasive behavioral data. Furthermore, we discuss the lessons learned from building TracM and discuss the application of the concept to other types of track-based services.

Keywords: Location, Privacy, Track-based services, Privacy-By-Substitution, Behavioral Features, Running.

1 Introduction

Recently, new types of Location-Based Services (LBSs) have emerged where the foundation of the service is a track - a time-ordered sequence of locations - rather than a single location. These services are called *track-based services* and include application domains, such as, ride-sharing, road-pricing, usage-based car insurance and sport trackers [5].

Ever since location technology appeared on the mass market in special purpose devices and mobile phones, the issue of location privacy has been raised [8]. For track-based services the problem is even more pertinent to address, as several kinds of personal information can be inferred from location tracks [8]. For instance, this raises issues with regards to citizen surveillance in connection with government-based road-pricing or customer surveillance for usage-based car insurances.

A recent survey of methods for location privacy identifies a general lack of methods for track-based services as most existing obfuscation and anonymity methods only consider point-of-interest services [6]. This lack of methods is also

A.U. Schmidt et al. (Eds.): MOBISEC 2012, LNICST 107, pp. 107–118, 2012.

noted by Ruppel et. al [12], who present some of the first attempts to obfuscate a track of locations. A study by Krumm [8] demonstrates the potential hazards in sharing large amounts of location data. Furthermore, three general privacy methods for track-based services are presented, but the methods suffer from potentially degrading service quality. Mun et. al [11] present the privacy method of selective hiding, but this method is only applicable to a limited set of track-based services. Furthermore, existing software infrastructures for supporting track-based services do not even address privacy explicitly [5,9].

In this paper we present the concept of *privacy by substitution* that addresses the problem without degrading service quality by substituting location tracks with less privacy invasive behavioral data extracted from raw tracks of location data or other sensing data. The behavioral data is then used instead of the location tracks to realise the intended application logic. Furthermore, by extracting the behavioral feature data on users' devices only less invasive data needs to be shared with external parties. We argue for that many possibilities exist for substituting location-tracks with less privacy invasive behavioral feature data to address the individual privacy needs of track-based services [13]. For example, in a running scenario we can extract behavioral features, such as height and pace curves, and length and completion times, which reveals much less information than a time-ordered sequence of locations. In a usage-based car insurance scenario one could extract features, such as, acceleration or deceleration patterns, as well as kilometers where speed limits are exceeded. It depends on the application scenario what data is relevant. In the following we list examples of highly invasive data one should avoid sharing and examples of less invasive data.

Highly Invasive: Location tracks, home or work address, own or family members identity, daily temporal patterns, social values.
Less Invasive: Altitude, pace, speed, bearing, mode of transportation, acceleration profile, accumulated road usage.

The contributions of this paper are as follows: (i) we present the concept of *privacy by substitution*; (ii) We explore this concept by designing and implementing *TracM*, a track-based community service for kids and youngsters to share and compare running performance to promote healthy behavior. We show how the service can be implemented substituting location tracks with less privacy invasive Decorated Height Curves (DHCs) and using similarity comparison techniques to realise the intended application logic; (iii) We present evaluation results for both simulated and real world running tracks that provide evidence that these techniques can compare a runner's performance and identify relevant runners / tracks to virtually compete against. The results indicate that a similarity technique based on normalized Euclidean distances gives the best comparison performance; (iv) Furthermore, we discuss the lessons learned from building TracM and discuss the application of the concept to other types of track-based services.

2   Using Less Invasive Behavioral Data

We explore a community service for runners with the intent to build a smartphone application for kids and youngsters to promote healthy behavior. The intended application is going to be launched by a national agency and therefore a requirement is that it provides protection of the kids' and youngsters' privacy. On the other hand it is known that social community aspects of smartphone applications can provide a strong motivational drive for behavioral change [10]. However, current methods for implementing such social community services require that complete location tracks are shared with external services which might be a problem, e.g., if a stalker can infer the location of a victim at a specific time of day. Therefore, there is a need to apply our concept in this scenario to substitute the sharing of location tracks with less privacy invasive behavioral data to improve the privacy protection while providing community driven functionality.

The three steps involved in applying our concept of privacy by substitution are as follows:

(i) Analyze the service's data requirements and functionality. (ii) Identify a minimal set of behavioral data that can fulfill the data needs of the service. E.g., for the running scenario we identified that decorated height curves can fulfill this need. (iii) Find means to implement the service functionality using behavioral data. E.g, in the running case use similarity techniques to compare decorated height curves and thereby realise the intended application logic.

For step one we have analysed existing track-based community services for runners [2,3] and identified three types of functionality (F1-F3) to support:

F1 - Share: Runners should be able to share their running performance results via social media, e.g., total distance and completion time.

F2 - Compete: Runners should be able to compete againts each other.

F3 - Inspire: Runners should be able to share tracks to inspire other runners to run new routes.

We will in the following sections cover step two and three and show how to implement **F2** and outline solutions for **F1** and **F3**, using behavioral features.

3   TracM - Behavioral Feature Extraction Services

Building on the previous analysis, we present TracM, a privacy preserving distributed service for implementing track-based social community services for runners. TracM provides privacy preserving implementations of functionality **F1-F3**. Smartphone applications, such as, the mentioned application for kids and youngsters can then be implemented using TracM by implementing a graphical user interface that utilize the TracM functionality. The two main techniques to implement the functionality are Decorated Height Curves (DHCs) and similarity techniques for comparing DHCs. Hence in relation to the principle of privacy by substitution, DHCs and comparison of these become the tool that facilitates the substitution.

Decorated Height Curves. consist of tuples of time, length, height and pace values. To compute a DHC TracM collects a regular time-stamped GPS location track which is then transformed into a DHC. A GPS track is transformed into a DHC in the following way:

$$(timestamp, latitude, longitude, altitude) \Rightarrow (time, length, height, pace)$$

The individual values in the tuples are calculated in the following way:

Time time since the user started running to add temporal privacy and therefore $time_0 = 0.0s$

Length distance moved since the user started running and is determined by the distance between consecutive GPS positions starting with $length_0 = 0.0m$.

Height normalized height h_r' of a GPS position, offset by the mean height h_{mean} over the whole location track. For the N height entries of a DHC each entry h_r is normalized as follows:

$$h_r' = h_r - \bar{a} \quad \wedge \quad \bar{a} = \frac{\sum_i^N h_i}{N}$$

Using the mean of maximum and minimum heights for normalization was also considered, but this created problems with erroneous height measurements as they could offset the curve making it different from similar curves with no errors.

Pace in meters per seconds are calculated from pairs of consecutive GPS positions.

The flow in TracM is as follows focusing on **F2: Compete**: (1) Initially the user either selects/creates a route in their own local collection or selects an inspiration height curve (HC) receiving good ranks by other runners provided by a remote DHC repository (**F3: Inspire**). In the later case the service will find the most similar local route, if it exists, matching the height profile and show it to the user. (2) The HC of the route is sent to a comparator which uses a similarity measure to find the most similar HC from the remote DHC repository. (3) This DHC is then sent to the local TracM service. The TracM service continually checks that the user is actually running along the route while informing the user of progress in relation to the DHC.

Track creation/selection and recording of the users track are both done on the TracM device and, hence, what is made publically available is only the HC in (2). Afterwards the user can share summary statistics including the height curve over relevant social media channels (**F1: Share**).

Characteristics of Similar Height Curves. A central element, in the above solutions, is to be able to compare HCs. For the comparison we define that two curves' similarity depend on the number of similarity criteria given below that they satisfy:

C1 nearly the same total ascent and total descent.

C2 peaks appear on similar places on the length axis. I.e. in a visual inspection of the curves they should peak at similar times on the length axis.

C3 close to similar minimum and maximum heights.

C4 Two curves which are similar in every aspect besides being shifted along the length axis, should have a high degree of similarity. This is to insure that if two users run the same track, and starts tracking with 20m between the start points they should still be detected as running on a similar track.

C5 Curves should be of similar length within a percentage threshold of $\Theta = \pm 10\%$.

C6 Two curves that only differ in being shifted on the height axis should be exactly similar.

3.1   Similarity Measures

The other main concept in TracM is the similarity between features based on DHCs. Two of the similarity measures we consider in this work are known from shape similarity [14] and the last three from statistics. From shape similarity the following similarity measures were implemented: *Euclidean Distance* and *Integral*. From statistics the following measures were implemented: *Cosine Coefficient, Histogram Intersection*, and *Kolmogorov-Smirnov*. For the three latter to make sense, one can think of the height values as the sample set. This requires that the height measurements are spaced equally apart on the length axis. Due to variations in running speed, positioning errors and sample jitter, DHCs from GPS tracks will not be evenly spaced. Therefore we process the DHCs using interpolation to have a height measurement for each twenty meters. It is a problem that some of the similarity measures require curves to have the same length. To adress this we extend the shortest curve by the length missing at the same height as the last measured height. Another option would be to just compare the curves until the shortest is finished, but this was rejected as it would have a significant impact if the route ends in a steep incline.

Euclidean Distance Measure. The Euclidean distance measure between two curves C and D is calculated as the sum of the Euclidean distance between the individual points c_i and d_i for i from 1 to N. We expand this measure by taking the K nearest points on the target curve into consideration and take the minimum distance. Furthermore, the result is normalized by the mean distance to be comparable for curves of different length:

$$E(K, C, D) = \frac{\sum_i^N min_k(\sqrt{(c_{k_x} - d_{k_x})^2 + (c_{k_x} - d_{k_y})^2})}{N}$$

Where min_k iterates from $i - K$ to $i + K$ and returns the minimum distance. The measure is referred to as $E(K)$.

Integral Measure. The Integral (Int) measure computes the area of symmetric difference of the area spanned by the two curves C and D and negative infinity, defined as

$$I(C, D) = area((C - D) \cup (D - C))$$

The output will be a positive number and the smaller it is, the more similar the curves are.

Cosine Coefficient. The Cosine (Cos) similarity measure captures the similarity between two vectors C and D by measuring the angle between them. It examines whether these point in relatively the same direction. In our case the vectors contain equally spaced height entries. The measure is calculated using the following formula:

$$cos(\theta) = \frac{C \cdot D}{\| C \| \| D \|}$$

Histogram Intersection. Histogram intersection (His) measures the distance between two histograms and is often used as a similarity measure for images.

$$H(C, D) = 1 - \frac{\sum_i min(c_i, d_i)}{\sum_i d_i}$$

Here C and D are the two sample sets of heights represented as histograms. The output is a number between zero and one with one denoting exactly similar curves.

Kolmogorov-Smirnov Distance. The Kolmogorov-Smirnov distance (KS), measures the similarity of two sample sets of heights C and D. It is defined as follows for each sample c_i and d_i:

$$K(C, D) = max_i|c_i - d_i|$$

4   Evaluation of Decorated Height Curve Similarity

To find a good similarity measure for DHCs to use for realising the intended application logic, an evaluation framework was developed to test TracM with each of the five aforementioned similarity measures. We consider two versions of the Euclidean metric with K equal to 1 and 10 named E(1) and E(10), respectively. It would be relevant in future work to consider other parameterisations of this metric.

For the evaluation we establish a ground truth using the characteristics from Section 3. To test $C1$, $C3$ and $C5$ statistics for the curves can be computed and compared. $C2$, $C4$ and $C6$ can be tested using visual inspection.

The evaluation is based on simulated as well as real world data. The length of the tracks is selected to be 5 km since the domain is running and 5 km is a distance most people feel comfortable running. According to $C5$, this gives us with our choice of Θ a range from 4.5 to 5.5 km in the real world data of tracks with should be considered similar.

4.1   Simulated Height Curves

The simulated curves are chosen to exercise most of the characteristics from Section 3. The basic set of simulated curves are listed in Table 1. All curves have a height difference of 100 m (except for the flat curve). Therefore $C3$ is always satisfied in the simulation cases.

Table 1. List of simulated curves

$flat$	A flat curve.
sin, sin^{-1}	A sine curve and it's inverse.
asc, des	A curve that evenly ascents from -50 m to 50 m during the entire track and it's inverse.
$peak$, val	A curve that evenly ascents from -50 m to 50 m and halfway descents from 50 m to -50 m evenly and it's inverse.
$peaks$	A curve that evenly ascents from -50 m to 50 m in 250 m and descents from -50 m to 50 m in 250 m. This pattern is repeated throughout the 5 km.

Some of the curves in addition have two shifted versions where they either start out with 500 m in the same height or end in 500 m in the same height (e.g. $peaks_b$ and sin_a). This is specifically to test the criteria $C4$.

For the evaluation using the simulated curves we select three test cases having very different shapes: $peak$, asc and $peaks$. The test cases are named by the source height curve:

Test Case: peak (S1) peak shares total ascent and descent with sin, sin^{-1}, val, $peak_b$, $peak_a$ and, therefore, $C3$ is satisfied. In relation to $C4$ $peak_b$ and $peak_a$ should turn out similar.

It is expected that the most similar curves are the shifted versions of $peak$ followed by sin and it's shifted versions. This is based on $C1$ and $C3$ and the fact that $peak$ and sin peak on the same place on the length axis ($C2$). The top 5 results of each similarity measure can be found in the table of Figure 1 in ascending order.

We notice that all measures agree that shifted versions of $peak$, and sin and it's shifted versions are the most similar as expected. The measures agree on similar curves, but disagree on order. In the figure we also see $peak$, $peak_{after}$, sin, and $flat$ visually. In relation to $C2$ the visual inspection indicate similarity of sin and $peak_{after}$ as they have similar peaks. However, $flat$, which was rated similar by the KS measure, is very dissimilar. Hence, KS is not a good measure in this case.

Test Case: ascent (S2) asc is characterized by having no descent, sharing that feature with $flat$ and sharing total descent with all other curves except $peaks$, $flat$ and des. Results can be found in Figure 2.

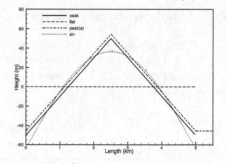

Cos	His	KS	Int	E(1)	E(10)
$peak_a$	sin	sin	$peak_a$	$peak_a$	$peak_a$
sin	$peak_a$	$peak_a$	sin	sin	sin
sin_a	sin_a	sin_a	sin_a	sin_a	sin_a
$peak_b$	sin_b	$flat$	$peak_b$	$peak_b$	$peaks_a$
sin_b	$peak_b$	$peaks$	sin_b	sin_b	$peaks$

Fig. 1. Table listing most similar curves to *peak* found by the similarity measures, and a subset of these shown visually

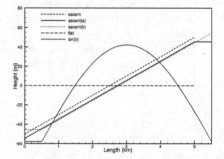

Cos	His	KS	Int	E(1)	E(10)
asc_a	asc_a	asc_a	asc_a	asc_a	asc_a
asc_b	asc_b	asc_b	asc_b	asc_b	asc_b
sin_b	sin_b	$peaks_b$	$flat$	$flat$	$peaks_b$
$peak_b$	$peak_b$	sin_b	$peak_b$	$peak_b$	$peaks$
$peaks_b$	$peaks_b$	$flat$	$peak$	$peaks_b$	$peaks_a$

Fig. 2. Table listing most similar curves to *asc* found by the similarity measures, and a subset of these shown visually

All measures agree on the two most similar curves being the shifted versions of *asc*. But besides from that the measures do not agree. In the figure the shifted versions of *asc* along with two of the other similar curves are shown. The visual inspection indicates that neither sin_b nor *flat* are similar to *asc*, and hence, the likely reason that the measures disagree is that there are no more than two similar curves. This is confirmed by the output from the measures, where there is a large gap in the values from the shifted curves of *asc* to the next.

Test Case: peaks (S3) peaks is characterized by the fact that shifting the curve by 500 m on the length axis has the consequence of producing a curve that is close to the inverse of the original while sharing total ascent/descent (C1), and it should be similar in relation to $C4$. The shifted versions of the curve should be similar in relation to $C2$. Results can be found in Figure 3.

All measures but KS agree that $peaks_a$ is the most similar, but from there on they differ a lot. However, three agree on *flat* as being the second most similar. In Figure 3, *peaks* and it's shifted versions along with *flat* and sin_a are shown. *peaks* and $peaks_{before}$ clearly demonstrate the issue described in $C4$. Hence, this curve has to be rated as similar. Only KS and E(10) rate $peaks_{before}$ among the top 5 similar curves and since KS rated *flat* as the most similar, only E(10) performs adequate according to $C4$.

Cos	His	KS	Int	E(1)	E(10)
$peaks_a$	$peaks_a$	$flat$	$peaks_a$	$peaks_a$	$peaks_a$
sin_a	$flat$	$peaks_a$	$flat$	$flat$	$peaks_b$
$peak_a$	sin	$peak$	val	$peak_a$	$peak_a$
des_b	sin_a	$peaks_b$	asc	des_b	$flat$
des_a	des_b	sin	$peak$	des_a	$peak_b$

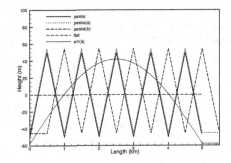

Fig. 3. Table listing most similar curves to *peaks* found by the similarity measures, and a subset of these shown visually

Overall, the more complex the curves become, the more different the measures perform. For S1 and S2 several measures solved the problem well, but in S3 only E(10) performed as expected. Furthermore, KS and His proved to perform significantly worse than the other measures and, hence, we will leave out their results in the following section as they proved to perform bad on real world data as well.

4.2 Real World Data

To gather data for the real world evaluation we use GPSies.com, a large database of GPS tracks, [4]. As TracM enables users to compete against users from other regions than their own, data from three countries is chosen: Germany, Denmark and The Netherlands. A query for 200 tracks was issued for each of these three countries, and from these 31 tracks were selected at random for comparison (labeled $t1$ to $t31$). In ten repetitions an input curve were selected, leaving a set of curves for comparison of size 30. To establish a ground truth the curves were manually compared by visual inspection to the remaining 30 curves with regards to the criteria $C1$-$C6$. The curves satisfying $C1$-$C6$ were marked as similar and therefore should be identified as similar by the evaluated metrics.

In the following we will discuss one of the test cases and list top 10 most similar curves for each measure. The considered curve is almost flat. Total ascent is 20 m, descent is 20 m, and the height difference is 4 m. Ground truth and result of the test case can be found in Table 2. Here we notice that Cos and E(10) perform good and Int and E(1) worse. Figure 4 shows the input curve, t30, in relation to a very similar curve, t15, and a dissimilar, t28.

Table 2. Ground truth and result of one repetition, with top 10 most similar curves for each measure. Numbers in parenthesis are curves not present in ground truth.

		1	2	3	4	5	6	7	8	9	10
Ground Truth	Cos	(t7)	t26	t20	t14	t15	(t24)	t4	t21	t3	(t11)
t3, t4, t14, t15,	Int	t14	t4	t15	(t24)	(t13)	(t10)	(t12)	(t25)	(t8)	(t22)
t20, t21, t26, t31	$E(1)$	t14	t4	t15	(t24)	(t8)	(t12)	(t13)	(t10)	(t25)	t26
	$E(10)$	t21	(t11)	t31	t4	t15	t14	(t19)	t26	t20	t3

Table 3. The average performance, taken over the ten tested curves, of the similarity measures by how many of the ground truth curves were found in the top 5 and top 10 results, respectively.

Test	Cos	Int	E(1)	E(10)
Top 5	64.5%	68.3%	68.3%	74.3%
Top 10	73.9%	72.3%	74.0%	91.1%

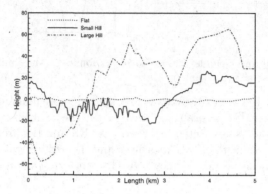

Fig. 4. Three curves from the real world test case

A summary of the results of all 10 test curves can be found in Table 3. Here we see accuracy of the different measures for top 5 and top 10 with respect to the ground truth set identified. As the results show, once again E(10) outperforms the other measures. However, even with this measure, some curves are classified incorrectly.

5   Performance and Potentials Beyond Running Tracks

We presented the concept of privacy by substitution. We evaluated this concept by developing, implementing, and evaluating TracM and showed that it is indeed possible to find less privacy invasive behavioral data to provide the functionality of a track-based community service for runners. I.e. with the current results it is indeed possible to create privacy enhanced services for kids and youngsters.

A limitation of our current implementation of TracM is that we did preprocessing when comparing two curves of unequal length, by choosing a naive strategy of prolonging the shorter curve with a flat piece based on last height. It would be relevant to explore how changing this strategy would effect the similarity. The measure E(10) had the best performance eventhough not flawless. Therefore as an additional element one could let the user check the proposed curve by visual inspection and select another if unsatisfied.

The advantage of the approach used in TracM, is that it is a concept that can be applied to a range of services. However, this also has the disadvantage that the method does not directly prescribe how to solve the privacy problem in a particular application as the choice of behavioral data and similarity measures have to meet the specific requirements of that application. To generalize the method, we will apply the method to several domain cases and hope to develop a toolkit to support developers in providing privacy based on feature extraction techniques.

As we illustrated with TracM it takes some effort to determine the behavioral data that should replace tracks. This is mainly due the fact that this was the first application domain to which the concept was applied, but also because it does require a different mindset overall. The case of community based track sharing for runners is, however, relatively easy compared to other domains as no large corporations or government agencies have to base their business on the functionality as they would have to in usage-based insurance or road pricing scenarios.

To explore the generally applicability for other application domains in track-based services, let us briefly examine usage-based insurance, of which the Alka Box [1] is an example. Currently, such systems are based on location tracks of the user, but instead of calculating insurance premium based on *where* the user has driven, it might make more sense to base it on *how* he drives. This is based on the assumption that, in car insurance, an aggressive driving style is more likely to capture how likely a user is to be in an accident rather than where he drives. The driving style might be estimated by analyzing features such as the acceleration/deceleration patterns in relation to speed, as well as the amount of kilometers where speed limits are exceeded, etc.. This leads to pattern matching and hence similarity measures can be used to solve the problem.

This indicates that this approach can also be used for other application domains in track-based services. However, actual implementations of such systems are needed to further evaluate the potential of the concept.

6 Conclusion

In this paper, we introduced the concept of privacy by substitution where less privacy invasive behavioral feature data is shared instead of complete location tracks to improve privacy. To apply the concept one has to identify the least amount of behavioral data needed to enable a specific track-based service and techniques for using the behavioral data to realise the intended application logic. We applied this concept to the domain of community-based running track sharing and design and implemented TracM, a service supporting feature extraction based on decorated height curves and similarity measures. Furthermore, we evaluated five similarity measures with TracM on simulated and real world data, and found that a normalized Euclidean distance had the best similarity performance. Furthermore, we argued that the concept has a more general applicability exemplified by usage-based insurance and road-pricing.

In our ongoing work we are trying to address the following: First, we will deploy the TracM service in the context of a mobile application to study whether users feel that it provides a similar service to existing services and if such a service can be efficiently implemented [7]. Second, we propose to explore the presented concept for other track-based services with emphasis on road-pricing and usage-based insurance. Finally, we propose to implement a wider array of similarity measures which can be used in adding privacy to track-based services.

Acknowledgments. This work is supported by a grant from the Danish Council for Strategic Research for the project: EcoSense.

References

1. Alka box (2012), http://www.alkabox.dk/
2. Endomondo (2012), http://www.endomodo.com/
3. Garmin connect (2012), http://connect.garmin.com/
4. Gpsies.com (2012), http://www.gpsies.com/
5. Ananthanarayanan, G., Haridasan, M., Mohomed, I., Terry, D., Thekkath, C.A.: Startrack: a framework for enabling track-based applications. In: Proc. of the 7th Int. Conf. on Mobile Systems, Applications, and Services (2009)
6. Andersen, M.S., Kjærgaard, M.B.: Towards a New Classification of Location Privacy Methods in Pervasive Computing. In: Puiatti, A., Gu, T. (eds.) MobiQuitous 2011. LNICST, vol. 104, pp. 150–161. Springer, Heidelberg (2012)
7. Kjærgaard, M.B.: Location-based services on mobile phones: Minimizing power consumption. IEEE Pervasive Computing 11(1), 67–73 (2012)
8. Krumm, J.: Inference Attacks on Location Tracks. In: LaMarca, A., Langheinrich, M., Truong, K.N. (eds.) Pervasive 2007. LNCS, vol. 4480, pp. 127–143. Springer, Heidelberg (2007)
9. Langdal, J., Schougaard, K.R., Kjærgaard, M.B., Toftkjær, T.: PerPos: A Translucent Positioning Middleware Supporting Adaptation of Internal Positioning Processes. In: Gupta, I., Mascolo, C. (eds.) Middleware 2010. LNCS, vol. 6452, pp. 232–251. Springer, Heidelberg (2010)
10. Mueller, F., Agamanolis, S.: Sports over a distance. Comput. Entertain. 3 (2005)
11. Mun, M., Reddy, S., Shilton, K., Yau, N., Burke, J., Estrin, D., Hansen, M., Howard, E., West, R., Boda, P.: Peir, the personal environmental impact report, as a platform for participatory sensing systems research. In: Proc. of the 7th Int. Conf. on Mobile Systems, Applications, and Services. ACM (2009)
12. Ruppel, P., Treu, G., Küpper, A., Linnhoff-Popien, C.: Anonymous User Tracking for Location-Based Community Services. In: Hazas, M., Krumm, J., Strang, T. (eds.) LoCA 2006. LNCS, vol. 3987, pp. 116–133. Springer, Heidelberg (2006)
13. Scipioni, M.P., Langheinrich, M.: I'm here! privacy challenges in mobile location sharing. In: 2nd Int. Workshop on Security and Privacy in Spontaneous Interaction and Mobile Phone Use, IWSSI/SPMU 2010 (2010)
14. Veltkamp, R.C.: Shape matching: similarity measures and algorithms. In: International Conference on Shape Modeling and Applications, SMI 2001, pp. 188–197 (May 2001)

Securing Data Privacy on Mobile Devices
in Emergency Health Situations

Kalpana Singh[1], Jian Zhong[2], Vinod Mirchandani[2], Lynn Batten[1], and Peter Bertok[2]

[1] School of Information Technology, Deakin University, Melbourne, Australia
[2] School of Computer Science, RMIT University, Melbourne Australia
{kalpana,lynn.batten}@deakin.edu.au,
{jian.zhong,vinod.mirchandani,peter.bertok}@rmit.edu.au

Abstract. When providing critical emergency care in a remote location, a local response team needs access to the patient's healthcare data. Such healthcare data is protected by privacy rules and laws in most jurisdictions. It is therefore a challenge to be able to provide the response team with the relevant data while protecting the privacy of that data. In this paper, we present a system designed to enhance privacy protection of sensitive data downloaded to a mobile client device from a remote server, such as in the case of accessing medical information in emergency situations.

Keywords: mobile device, privacy, security, health data, emergency.

1   Introduction

The evolution of mobile technology has facilitated remote access to various databases. There are established methods to protect the data while in transit, but protecting data on the user device is still an issue [1]. A major challenge is that mobile equipment can easily fall into the wrong hands, while the often limited resources make data protection difficult. Health-related data frequently needs access from remote locations, such as for out-of-hospital care or in emergency scenarios, and maintaining the privacy of data downloaded to a mobile device is an essential requirement [2], [3], [4]. This paper describes a solution that provides a good level of privacy protection of downloaded data at affordable cost and provides more security features than previous work in the literature. In particular, our solution:

- enforces privacy at the user end
- authenticates the mobile hardware, the software running on it and the user
- has a flexible, and so scalable, architecture provided by a modular approach.

We integrate data privacy techniques in a novel way with classical security methods including encryption and one-time-passwords. At the user end, this gives us the capability of preventing the unwanted file-related functions of copying, saving and re-distribution of the file.

In subsequent sections, we discuss the relevant literature, and describe the proposed architecture with its components. We also compare our model to similar solutions.

A.U. Schmidt et al. (Eds.): MOBISEC 2012, LNICST 107, pp. 119–130, 2012.

2   The Relevant Literature

The literature on the use of mobile phones in connection with patient medical data falls broadly into three categories: there is the use for chronic care patient monitoring (e.g. [5]) the use to provide services to patients (e.g. [3], [4], [6]) and the use to obtain patient information in an emergency setting (e.g. [2], [7]). We discuss these three applications here, but will emphasize the last application as this is the area in which our paper offers something new.

Chronic and Aftercare Patient Monitoring. In [5], the authors consider the situation of a patient whose vital signs must be constantly monitored. The use of a mobile phone, in conjunction with Bluetooth and GSM, to do this monitoring is promoted for this purpose because it permits the patient flexibility of movement and the ability to live at home. The system was tested on a small group of heart patients and evaluated for reliability, performance and quality.

Providing Services to Patients. Whether hospitalized or not, many people need access to health care services to access medical records, buy prescriptions, or send images to a medical professional for advice. Weerasinghe et al. ([3]) present a 3-phase protocol for providing secure transmissions between patients and healthcare services over a mobile network. The phases include authenticating connections between the mobile station and each of a health care operator and a health care service provider, and the construction of data access levels in the service provider to determine who deals with the request from the patient. They explain how the security of the architecture of [3] can be implemented by means of a 'security capsule' embedded in the mobile device. We examine this capsule and its interaction with other components of the architecture in Section 4.

In [6], the authors explain their design of a "mobile-phone-based information display for emergency department patients" and how they tested this on a group of twenty-five patients in an emergency department along with the patients' families. Their motivating argument is that the emergency department environment would be improved if patients were kept informed of their treatment and health status and were able to share this with their families. Medical records were pulled from the hospital network and used to populate mobile phone displays in real time. Since the patients' own mobile phones were used, they had private access to their personal health information regardless of their location. The authors concluded that "this is a promising approach to improving patient awareness".

Emergency Setting. The afore-mentioned papers [1] and [7] also consider the situation when the patient needs critical emergency care and it is a local emergency response team that needs access to the patient healthcare data. In both of these papers, there is a focus on authenticating the emergency team and their request for information, and on preserving the privacy of the patient data sent to the team. In Section 4 of this paper, we compare our proposed architecture with theirs in detail.

Mirkovic et al. also consider this situation in their work in [2]; their architecture is similar to that of Weerasinghe et al. in that in both cases, separation of zones is used as a security measure at the server end. However, in [1] and [7], tokens are issued in order to establish trust between the communicating parties while this is replaced by the use of Public Key Infrastructure certificates in [2]. We also compare our proposed architecture with this paper in detail in Section 4. Finally, we refer the reader to an earlier paper [8], where the authors also consider the emergency setting but the focus is on maintaining the privacy of patient data rather than the use of mobile phones. The privacy component of the architecture in that earlier paper has been imported into the current proposal.

In Section 4, we examine several of these papers primarily from the point of view of the mobile user and compare features in Table 1.

3   Proposed Model

Our system was designed for enhanced privacy protection of sensitive data downloaded to a mobile client device from a remote server, such as in the case of accessing medical information in emergency situations. The data server is not part of our system; any data sent to it (such as authentication data) or obtained from it (such as medical data) is not interpreted by the system described in this paper.

Our full architecture includes several clients, all accessing the one server. To simplify the explanations, in the system model here we present only one client, as shown in Figure 1. The client can be a resource-constrained remote device (RCRD), such as a smartphone, tablet PC or a laptop, with limited battery life, low computational power, and moderate storage capacity. On the server side, a Trust Server (TS) handles the security and privacy aspects, and every transfer between the client and the data server is under the control of the TS. The server side is assumed to have no threats from the inside; we provide protection only against external attacks.

To secure the connection, the participants are authenticated and the connection is protected. We perform authentication on three levels: device, software and user. First, the device is authenticated by checking its ID, such as the IMEI number for 3G phones or MAC address for WiFi connections. Then, the client side has to send a preliminarily agreed port-knocking code to prove that it is running the appropriate software. Finally, the user has to perform an ordinary login procedure.

We provide data protection both during transit and in the end-user device. TLS (http://tools.ietf.org/html/rfc5246) protects the data while traveling across networks; it was chosen because it is widely available and provides interoperability between different platforms. We provide additional confidentiality and privacy protection in the application layer to cater for the mobile nature of the client device.

In the following subsections, we describe the components of our architecture.

3.1   Client-Side Modules

We have augmented the RCRD with a proxy module to provide security and privacy protection. The RCRD proxy operates in conjunction with a proxy module in the TS.

(See Figure 1.) We do not show the applications communicating with the data server here, except for the user interface part that our system makes use of.

User interface. The user interface is our system's only visible part to the user. It is used for inputting user authentication data, which is forwarded to the TS. All other modules of the system are transparent, i.e. are not visible to the user.

RCRD proxy module. The Proxy performs three major tasks in the system. It (i) filters URLs and IP addresses for outgoing connections, (ii) builds and maintains a secure connection to the Trust Server and (iii) provides privacy protection to data downloaded into the client device. The RCRD proxy does not interact with the user and its operation is transparent to the end user, to facilitate operation when the user has to concentrate on other, vital tasks, as is the case in medical emergencies.

It has three sub-modules: the request filtering unit (RFU), the secure connection builder (SCB), and the file privacy enforcer (FPE); each sub-module corresponds to one of the three functions listed above.

RFU sub-module. The Request Filtering Unit performs simple access control for connection requests. For outgoing requests, it checks if connections are allowed to be set up to the URL or IP address of the remote peer mentioned in the request, and if yes, what sort of connection needs to be set up; for example it may need data confidentiality (encryption) or privacy protection.

Incoming connection requests are also filtered, to prevent links to unknown (and possibly rogue) peers. As the mobile device is likely to be used by various legitimate users, this is a basic protection against unintended use.

SCB sub-module. The user-to-data server communication has to go through a secure communication channel, to protect the data. Building up this channel starts with a three-level authentication. On the device level, the RCRD is authenticated to the Trust server by forwarding its ID. Next, on the software level we employ a port-knocking mechanism, in which the client module automatically sends a preliminarily agreed code to the Trust Server. If the code is correct, the Trust Server will accept the incoming connection request, and a communication channel with TLS protection is built up between the RCRD and the Trust Server. The port-knocking code is calculated separately on both sides, and it requires synchronization of the clocks on the client and server sides to some degree.

Upon successful completion of device and software authentication, a third authentication on the user level takes place, and this time the messages go through the TLS connection established earlier. On the client side the user is asked to enter a username that is forwarded, to the TS. Upon receiving the login request, the TS generates a one-time password (OTP) and sends it to the user via a different channel (SMS). The user has to enter this password, and the SCB sub-module sends it back to the TS. If the TS receives the correct password, communication via the connection will be enabled. If the password is not correct or does not reach the TS within a specific amount of time, the connection is closed. Each login attempt triggers the generation of a new password. The password is sent to the phone number registered against the username in the TS. Users are required to use a mobile phone separate from the RCRD itself; this is likely to be their usual personal mobile. We increased protection by requiring two devices, the RCRD and a mobile phone for successful authentication. We assume that they do not fall into the wrong hands at the same time. If the RCRD is compromised, the legal user still gets notification about each login attempt via the reception of a new password. As both generation and checking of the OTP take place on the server side, the user does not need to carry extra devices for generating the password, and the password-generating algorithm can be changed without notifying any of the other participants.

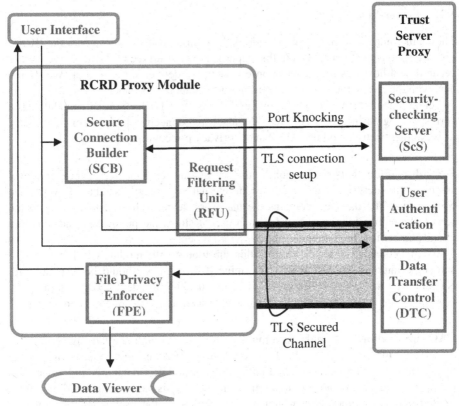

Fig. 1. System Architecture: The Client Side

FPE sub-module. The proxy monitors all data transfer of the established connection, and if a file of a particular data type (e.g. pdf) arrives from the server, the privacy-enforcer module will be activated. The purpose of the FPE sub-module is to ensure security and privacy of the protected information by not allowing certain operations in the associated data viewer which could lead to unauthorized access, such as copy or save. The data received from the server is in encrypted form and is stored in that form to provide protection within the mobile device as well. It is decrypted only for display. Furthermore, the FPE will erase the data from local memory (including the cache) in the RCRD after the user exits the data viewer.

Data sent by the TS and is encrypted using AES (key length: 256 bits); decryption is done at the user side in the FPE. Our implementation uses Java 1.6.0 with file handlers for jpeg and pdf files and Java Cryptographic Architecture for AES. (For more details see Section 5.)

The FPE module is also a placeholder for enhanced privacy-protection, such as additional algorithms to improve both security and data usability at the same time.

3.2   Server-Side Modules

The main component on the server side is the data repository whose data the RCRD user wants to access. Our focus in this paper is how the source of the access request is verified, and how this server's response is securely delivered to the user. We do not deal with the data server's internal working or its data in this paper.

Server side security is provided by our Trust Server. Each client-side module has a corresponding partner on the server side: a secure connection building module (ScS), a user authentication module (AUC) and a privacy protection module (DTC).

ScS sub-module. This sub-module is the server-side implementer of the three-level authentication described earlier. It uses an internal, user-profile database to verify the components. The database contains the hardware devices allowed to connect to the server, the authorized users, and for each user it stores the public key and a mobile phone number to which the one-time password is sent.

When a connection request reaches this sub-module, the module will remain silent and some internal processing will determine if the request should be responded to. Namely, first the client device is validated by checking the device ID, then the port-knocking code is verified. Upon positive authentication a TLS connection is set up.

UAC sub-module. User authentication is performed by sending a message asking for a username to the client via the TLS connection. After receiving the username, the phone number of the user is looked up in the sub-module's database, and a one-time password is generated and sent to the user via SMS. This password is valid only for a limited period of time, after which it is discarded. If the user authentication was successful before the wait timed out, the connection becomes operational, and this sub-module passes the connection on to the Data Transfer sub-module. Otherwise, the client is disconnected.

DTC sub-module. Any data transfer between the data server and the outgoing server port is controlled. The data obtained from the data server is examined before being sent over, and certain data types are encrypted before being sent to the RCRD client. For bulk data encryption we use secret-key encryption (AES), and the encryption key for each session is sent to the other side by using the public key of the client-side user.

3.3   Protocol Operation

The flow of messages in our protocol is shown in Fig. 2. The protocol starts with authentication in two steps: device authentication followed by user authentication. In the first step the RCRD proxy sends out the agreed port-knocking code immediately followed by a TLS connection request (client_hello). If a valid client device ID and the correct port-knocking code are received, the TS accepts the connection request and a TLS connection is set up.

In the second step, the user is asked to enter the username via the user interface, which is forwarded to the server side via the TLS connection. The TS then generates a one-time password and sends it to the user via SMS. The user has to enter this

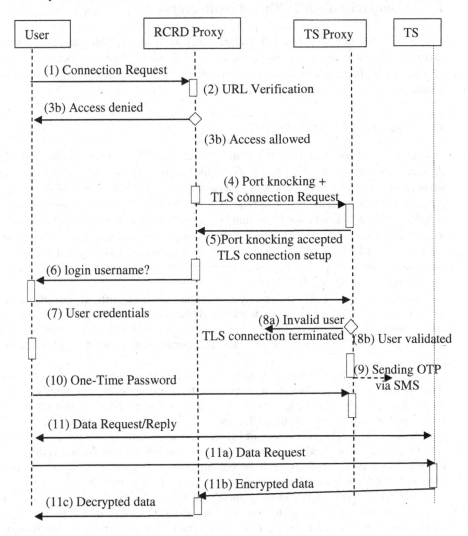

Fig. 2. Flow Diagram of the Proposed Protocol

password, which will be forwarded to the server. If the correct password is returned to the TS, the user is considered to have been authenticated, and the proxy will relay data between the user and the data server in both directions. At the end of the session, the client logs out by exiting the data viewer, and this results in closing the TLS connection. There is a maximum inactive connection time as well, after which the server automatically disconnects the client. This provides safety when the user forgets to log out, a frequently occurring scenario in emergency cases.

The server-side proxy also monitors the type of the data to be sent, and certain data types are encrypted before being forwarded to the client.

4   Comparison with Other Architectures

In Section 2, we mentioned several papers which built architectures to deal with an environment similar to ours: a low-resource device is used in a remote location to pull private patient information from a server. Here, we compare that work with our architecture as described in Section 3.

4.1   The work of Mirkovic et al.

The authors of [2] propose an architecture for securing mobile access to data from an electronic health record system. A made-for-purpose application is installed in advance on the mobile device but is independent of the device and mobile service provider. In their implementation, a request from a user to the health service provider is forwarded to an identity server to confirm user identity, and subsequently, the user request is forwarded to the authentication provider for authentication. While they indicate an SMS PIN push, which the user uses to generate an encrypted challenge, the resulting one-time-password generation at the authentication provider end was not actually implemented in their scheme.

Thus, the user is identified by means of an organization identifier (for example, the medical service in which the user works) and the mobile device is identified by a subscription number to a GSM or UMTS mobile network. The user must also be registered with the health service provider, the identity server and the authentication provider.

The communication protocol operation needs a user to communicate with *three different servers* in [2], while in our approach, the user deals directly only with one server (the Security-checking Server). The use of three servers rather than one increases the opportunity available for slowing down the operation of the overall system. In addition the architecture of [2] lacks a mechanism for file processing after data has been downloaded from the server to the mobile device. In our system, we prevent file-related functions such as copying, saving or distribution of the file; moreover, the file is erased from the cache as soon as the user exits it.

While the authors of [2] identify their mobile device by means of a network subscription number and registration with the identity server, in addition to such identification, we authenticate the device by means of a port knocking mechanism. (See Section 3.1.)

4.2   The Work of Weerasinghe et al.

We focus particularly here on the paper [1] in which there is a detailed description of a 'security capsule' embedded in the mobile device. In fact, it is the authentication service in their architecture that installs this capsule in the mobile device. It is assumed that the capsule is secure, while the mobile device is susceptible to attacks. A password is used to gain access to the mobile device. The security capsule can store encrypted data and is also used to authenticate the device to other parties and to encrypt communication channels between the device and other parties. Only encrypted data is stored in the security capsule, and it is decrypted there on user request. The data interface on the mobile device cannot be changed or saved.

Authentication of the mobile device and user to the healthcare operator is based on a member ID, a OTP, some key material provided through a second channel and a token which is encrypted and includes a time-stamp [3]. This is similar to the scheme of [2] (although the authors of [2] implemented it without their equivalent of the key material). Weerasinghe et al [3] point out that the use of a time-stamp prevents a replay attack; this is also true with the use of a OTP. In their architecture, the communications used in authenticating the mobile device are encrypted using symmetric encryption. Once the authentication is given, the healthcare operator provides a public/private key pair to the user and then any confidential patient data is sent using the private key of the patient; this is the fundamental privacy-preserving mechanism used in this architecture.

4.3   Comparison Based on Architecture Attributes

Table 1 compares our proposed architecture with those of several authors on the basis of privacy and security features, as well as flexibility and transparency. A modular structure of an architecture provides it with flexibility for adaptation to varied environments and also with the ability to scale with the client base, and so we list modularity as one of the valuable features of an architecture designed to provide a user with data as a service.

We also consider the security of the communication mechanisms and apply weightings to the security provided. For **password security**, Level 0 refers to no passwords used at all; Level 1 refers to a user-generated password or one generated by any participant and not changed regularly; Level 2 refers to a regularly refreshed OTP supplied to the user from the server end. For **access security**, Level 0 refers to the use of an organizational ID; Level 1 refers to the generation and use of a OTP as well as organization ID; Level 2 refers to those mechanisms used in Level 1 as well as a second, independent OTP or password generation provided by a means different from that used for the first OTP. (In our architecture, the port knocking pattern is the second OTP.) For **data security**, Level 0 refers to no use of encryption; Level 1 refers to the use of encryption on either the channels used or the data being communicated; Level 2 refers to the use of encryption on both the channels used and the data being communicated.

Table 1. Comparison of key attributes of architectures in the literature with our proposed architecture

References ----------- Attributes	Singh [8]	Vardoulakis et al [6]	Weerashinghe et al [7]	Mirkovic et al [2]	Proposed Model
Password Security Level	2	1	2	2	2
Access Security Level	1	1	2	1	2
Data Security Level	2	1	2	2	2
Privacy Control	Middleware based limited privacy control	Data deletion	Encryption with public keys.	Out of band OTP transfer for access control	File management; out of band OTP transfer
Module structure of architecture	N/A	N/A	Yes	Yes	Yes
Transparent to User	With limitations	Yes	Yes	Yes	Yes
System implemented?	No	Yes	No	Yes	Yes

5   Experimental Results

Our experiments focused on the mobile device end and the communication between client and server. We used an HTC Wildfire phone (Android OS, internal storage: 146 MB, additional SD & phone storage: 1.7 GB), and measured the speed of the client-server connection, with and without port-knocking, decryption time for pdf and jpg files with AES on the RCRD and decryption time with an RSA private key of short keystrings, also on the RCRD.

Client-server connection speed. In the experiment, we launched 20 login requests and calculated the average time to connect. Both RCRD and TS were running on the same machine to minimize the effect of network conditions on the results. Moreover, we deleted the step of sending the OTP in an SMS to eliminate external factors such as human reaction time and phone network latency in the tests. The experiments were run on a laptop with Intel Dual core P7300 and 2G Ram, running Windows 7 with Visual Studio .NET 2010 Ultimate and included an SQL Server.

The average login time was 3.16 sec from clicking on the login button to the display of the requested page; performing port knocking added 0.82 sec to this.

Table 2. Encryption/Decryption time and speed of .pdf and .jpg files (AES 256-bit key)

File Size (KB)	File format	Encryption time (msec)	Decryption time (msec)	Encryption speed (KB/msec)	Decryption speed (KB/msec)
55	pdf	24.78	22.56	2.219	2.438
	jpg	138.24	136.99	0.398	0.401
110	pdf	32.81	31.80	3.353	3.459
	jpg	205.57	203.22	0.535	0.541
333	pdf	64.24	62.89	5.184	5.295
	jpg	350.82	347.89	0.949	0.957
685	pdf	80.89	79.02	8.468	8.669
	jpg	410.21	408.16	1.669	1.678
890	pdf	98.12	96.88	9.071	9.187
	jpg	530.22	528.07	1.679	1.685

AES decryption on RCRD. We implemented AES decryption with a key length of 256 bits. To see the effect on a relatively slow mobile device, in this experiment we used a laptop with Intel (R) Core (TM) i5 CPU M 430, 2.27 GHz. We used Java 2 Platform Micro Edition (J2ME) cryptography library [9] with BouncyCastle for the AES encryption and decryption. The RCRD was emulated on an Android emulator 4.0.3 (*API Level:* **15**) using Eclipse indigo 3.7.0 (http://www.eclipse.org/) on a Windows 7 (64 bit) operating system and with 3.00 GB of RAM.

The main goal was to compare the decryption times on the RCRD of the two file formats pdf and jpeg. The results are shown in Table 2. In the experiments, we considered file sizes ranging from 55 kb to 890 kb of text and image data, and averaged over 15 runs. The jpg files were significantly more costly to manage than the pdf files.

RSA decryption on RCRD. Because the AES key is sent encrypted with the receiver's public RSA key, we measured the decryption times of small strings of ciphertext. As the keys were regularly changed, we used short keys: the encryption key used was 18 bits; the decryption key was 8 bits. Encryption and decryption times for 256 bits of data, for example, were on average 0.0584 and 0.0438 secs respectively.

6   Summary and Conclusions

In this paper we proposed a solution for accessing health-care data from a mobile device in a secure manner. Security was provided by authenticating the participants: equipment, software and user. First, the device ID is checked against a list of authorized RCRDs, eliminating requests from rogue devices. The software must be able to generate a port-knocking code, and, combined with the device ID-check, this protects the server from port scanning and denial of service attacks. The user must be able to provide a one-time password. Using a OTP instead of prearranged passwords improves usability as well as efficiency for a health-care worker in an emergency scenario. To introduce additional security, a second device is involved, but rather than having a separate OTP generator, we assume the availability of a phone carried by the user. Using a separate channel (SMS) makes eavesdropping more difficult, and, in addition, users get SMS notification if someone is trying to access the server by using their login name. As the OTP is generated and checked by the same module, there is no need for password synchronization between different modules.

The modular architecture allows additional, privacy-preserving features. The data is stored in encrypted form on the RCRD, and is decrypted only for display. This prevents usable data from being left on the device unintentionally, an often occurring scenario in an emergency. We also provide limited protection against intentional misuse as we turn off data saving and manipulating options in the data viewer. Protecting the screen from being photographed, however, was beyond the scope of the project.

Our work has demonstrated the feasibility of providing private patient health data to medical emergency teams with resource-constrained devices in locations remote from the server while adhering to relevant privacy policies or laws.

References

1. Weerasinghe, D., Rajarajan, M., Rakocevic, V.: Device Data Protection in Mobile Healthcare Applications. In: Weerasinghe, D. (ed.) eHealth 2008. LNICST, vol. 1, pp. 82–89. Springer, Heidelberg (2009)
2. Mirkovic, J., Bryhni, H., Ruland, C.: Secure solution for mobile access to patient's health care record. In: Proc. of e-Health Networking, Applications and Services, pp. 296–303. IEEE Press (2011)
3. Weerasinghe, D., Elmufti, K., Rajarajan, M., Rakocevic, V.: Securing electronic health records with novel mobile encryption schemes. Int. J. Electronic Healthcare 3, 395–416 (2007)
4. Weerasinghe, D., Rajarajan, M., Elmufti, K., Rakocevic, V.: Patient privacy protection using anonymous control techniques. Methods Inf. Med 47, 235–240 (2008)
5. Yousef, J., Lars, A.: Validation of a real-time wireless telemedicine system using bluetooth protocol and a mobile phone for remote monitoring patient in medical practice. Eur. J. Med. Res. 10, 254–262 (2005)
6. Vardoulakis, L., Karlson, A., Morris, D., Smith, G., Gatewood, J., Tan, D.: Using mobile phones to present medical information to hospital patients. In: Proc. of CHI 2012, pp. 1411–1420. ACM Press (2012)
7. Weerasinghe, D., Rajarajan, M.: Secure trust delegation for sharing patient medical records in a mobile environment. In: Proc. of WiCOM 2011, pp. 1–4. IEEE-Wiley (2011)
8. Singh, K., Zhong, J., Batten, L., Bertok, P.: An efficient solution for privacy-preserving secure remote access to sensitive data. In: International Conference of Advanced Computer Science & Information Technology (submitted)
9. Hook, D.: Beginning Cryptography with Java. Wrox press, Wiley & Sons Inc., Hoboken, NJ (2005)

Author Index

Printed in the United States
By Bookmasters